AN HISTORIAN IN THE TWENTIETH CENTURY

# AN HISTORIAN
## IN THE
# TWENTIETH CENTURY

*Chapters in Intellectual Autobiography*

MAX BELOFF FBA

YALE UNIVERSITY PRESS

NEW HAVEN AND LONDON · 1992

# To Judith and Carol

Set in Goudy Old Style by Best-set Typesetter Ltd., Hong Kong
Printed and bound in Great Britain by The Bath Press, Avon

**Library of Congress Cataloging-in-Publication Data**

Beloff, Max, 1913–
    An historian in the twentieth century: chapters in intellectual autobiography / Max Beloff.
        p.    cm.
    Includes bibliographical references and index.
    ISBN 0–300–05743–1
    1. Beloff, Max, 1913–    .   2. Historians—Great Britain—
Biography.   3. Historiography—History—20th century.   4. History,
Modern—20th century—Historiography.   I. Title.
D15.B38A3   1992
941.082'092—dc20                                    92–13127
                                                         CIP


A catalogue record for this book is available from the British Library.

# Contents

# Acknowledgements

I wish to thank Francis Graham for turning my own typescript into a readable form, Mr Peter James for very helpful copy-editing, Mr A. S. Bell for solving a bibliographical problem, and above all, Robert Baldock of Yale University Press, without whose encouragement the book would never have been brought to a conclusion.

As always my thanks are due to the librarians and staffs of the Bodleian Library, the Codrington Library, the Library of the House of Lords, the Library of the University of Buckingham, the London Library and on this occasion the first library I used, the Library of St Paul's School.

Max Beloff
January 1992

# Introduction

Si haute que je remonte dans mes souvenirs, je me retrouve historien de plaisir ou de désir, pour ne point dire de coeur et de vocation.

Lucien Febvre

I cannot claim to be certain that my earliest memories reveal me already committed to becoming an historian, but I can say that I do not remember a time when I seriously thought of embarking upon an alternative career. In reviewing what I have actually done in my capacity as an historian, I have also to answer the question which a glance at the bibliography at the end of this volume will fortify, why I have seemingly darted from subject to subject while most of those describing how they entered the profession can point to the circumstances which led them to choose what turned out to be a lifetime of devotion to a single period or theme.[1] Most of the choices I made can, as I shall show, be put down to the vagaries of chance. Some were perhaps due to my upbringing and education, preparing me for or predisposing me to some choices rather than others.

My parents were Russian-speaking Jews who migrated to Britain around 1900; I myself was born in London in 1913 and was educated in London with English as my first language. My parents might be described as orthodox Jews but with a fairly lax degree of observance. I did acquire some familiarity with basic Jewish patterns of religious commitment, and accepted that this meant some distance from my non-Jewish contemporaries. But since my parents' social circle consisted of families very like themselves, I never felt part of the 'Anglo-Jewry' whether of the Orthodox or assimilated variety.

I do not think in retrospect that I got all that I might have done out of my family and its background and connections. I had

1.  See e.g. Pierre Nora ed. *Essais d'égo-histoire*, (Paris: 1987).

the notion that history was what one obtained from books and not by interrogating the living about their experiences. I did get some idea from my father about life in the small towns of the Jewish Pale of Settlement which were to be destroyed by the Holocaust; but I never brought myself to press my mother on what it had been like to be a Jewish woman student at the University of St Petersburg around the turn of the century. The advantage I did derive from my home background was the notion, still unfamiliar in this country, that it is perfectly normal to be able to converse in a number of languages. It was a fairly polyglot household – my parents spoke Russian to each other – but one might also hear German and Yiddish among their guests. Having to learn Hebrew for religious purposes as well as Latin and Greek, then still part of any respectable education, I was under some pressure where modern languages were concerned, having no particular gift in that direction. Chance had some influence on the outcome, in this case my health. I was sent for one winter at the age of fifteen or so to school in Switzerland, and the drilling in French I received over some six months has helped to make me impatient with those who believe that we can learn our own language properly with no attention to the rules of grammar.

It is perhaps also worth recording that the family was politically aware and that, from the earliest years I can remember, public events vied with cricket scores for my juvenile attention: general elections from 1922 on and events on the continent.

Indifferent health meant that I had a good deal of time on my hands in which reading was the only available occupation, television being unknown and radio in its infancy. I must assume that some of my later tastes and attitudes were influenced by the kind of historical works that were easily available to a schoolboy in the early 1920s, such as H. B. Marshall's *Our Island Story, Our Empire Story* – good patriotic stuff not likely to find favour with today's primary-school teachers. Historical fiction also played its part – was the distinction between fact and fiction clear in my mind? In this realm, Scott and Dumas were supreme, but one must add works by lesser mortals: Jane Porter's *Scottish Chiefs*, Charles Kingsley's *Westward Ho!* and Harrison Ainsworth's *The Tower of London*, not to speak of the innumerable novels by G. A. Henty – *With Moore at Corunna, With Kitchener in the Soudan* and so on.[2]

2.  Since today's schoolchildren read much less – television and videos are the foundations of illiteracy – it is easy to forget what an impact early read-

My early years at St Paul's School were mainly devoted to remedying, not altogether successfully, my weakness in Latin and Greek; I did acquire some rudiments of ancient history. But my serious interest in the subject must be dated from my entry into History Eighth, where I came under that most dynamic of schoolmasters, Philip Whitting, so many of whose pupils not only won open awards to Oxford and Cambridge but went on in their turn to become teachers of history in schools and universities.[3] My interest in politics took second place to the demands of study, but was not abandoned. Having secured in the autumn term of 1931 my place at Oxford, I took the next term off to go to Germany to learn the language, and so found myself in Berlin as the fortunes of the Weimar Republic were sinking and the Nazi star was in the ascendant.

While I spent most of my time working at my books in Berlin, I did some travelling as well and finished up in Danzig (now Gdansk), where a family connection had brought me in earlier years. Nowhere in Germany could one avoid the impact of politics, domestic and international. I wrote up my observations for the school magazine – on rereading the piece I think it is the best thing I ever wrote – and concluded by drawing a contrast between the glowering clouds of war and civil strife on the continent and what appeared to be the unconquerable complacency of England.[4]

Yet, when I went up to Oxford as an undergraduate in the autumn of 1932, what I had called in my article 'the fool's paradise' of 'our ancient seats of learning' took me into its embrace, and while I played some part in undergraduate politics my energies as at school were mainly channelled into my historical studies. Since my area of concentration under Whitting had been the nineteenth century, I decided to branch out into fields previously outside my range, so my undergraduate years were devoted to the Middle Ages and the Stuart period in England and my first research to the late seventeenth century, under the

ing can have on one's subsequent intellectual make-up. For an excellent example, see Chapter 3, 'Dream Kingdoms', in David Cairns's splendid *Berlioz*, vol. 1 (London: 1989).

3. The abolition of open scholarships and exhibitions by the Oxford and Cambridge colleges was one of the many foolish sacrifices made by the ancient universities to the fashionable egalitarianism of recent decades. It was a major blow to schoolboy scholarly ambitions.
4. Max Beloff, 'Return Journey', *The Pauline* (Summer 1932).

direction of a remarkable scholar and teacher, G. N. (later Sir
George) Clark.

It might thus have looked as though I had settled into a
conventional mainstream historian's career, and I was indeed
appointed to the staff of the history department at the University
of Manchester as a seventeenth-century specialist. Again, chance
stepped in. Having spent the year 1940–1 in the army, I found
the university on my return committed to doing something about
the history of the United States, which became central to my
teaching duties at Manchester and later when I went back to
Oxford in 1946.

As if this diversion were not enough, another presented itself.
The Royal Institute of International Affairs, which I had joined in
1937, was concerned during the war years with looking ahead
to the shape of the post-war world. In February 1941, it had
established a Committee on Reconstruction to co-ordinate such
activities, and the committee itself decided to proceed through a
number of study groups dealing with particular aspects of the
inquiry. In June that year, a study group on Anglo-Russian relations was set up and I was, at the suggestion of G. N. Clark,
appointed as its historical adviser to prepare papers for discussion
at the group's meetings. By the summer of 1944, the group's
work was complete but, given the delicate state of Anglo-Soviet
relations, a formal report was thought unwise. I was thus asked to
summarize the group's findings in a lecture at Chatham House
which was subsequently published.[5] Of more importance as far as
my historical interests were concerned was the way my work for
the group developed into my history of Soviet foreign policy.[6]

The years during which I was back in Oxford (1946–74) teaching American history, and later on British government and
aspects of imperial and international affairs, were the most single-
hearted in respect of my commitment to historical research and
writing, and hence the most productive. Again, however, when
I could have been looking forward to an even more productive retirement, chance took a hand. I got involved in the
controversies about educational standards in the 1960s and was

5.  Max Beloff, 'Some Aspects of Anglo-Soviet Relations', *International Affairs*,
    XXI (April 1945).
6.  Max Beloff, *The Foreign Policy of Soviet Russia*, vol. 1: *1929–1936* (London:
    1947), vol. 2: *1936–1941* (London: 1949).

drawn into the group which had decided that it would be useful to have a university in this country outside the state-financed framework and able to experiment in ways increasingly unavailable to a system which was becoming more and more unified. As a result, I found myself principal-designate of the University College of Buckingham, now the University of Buckingham. Trying to get a fledgling university on its feet was hard to combine with serious historical research.[7]

This incursion into academic administration had another consequence. It changed my political orientation. At school I had been a Conservative, as a student a socialist, after the war a Liberal, of a mildly active kind. The bitter hostility of the Labour government to the project of an independent university and the failure of the Liberals (then moving increasingly to the left) to give it any support inclined me to move towards the Conservatives, though as the head of a university institution I felt that all party-political activity was probably undesirable. When at the end of 1979 I retired, it became understandable that I should join the Conservative Party, and when at the beginning of 1981 Mrs Margaret Thatcher, who had been a stalwart and invaluable supporter of Buckingham, asked me to go to the House of Lords on the Conservative ticket, I had no hesitation about accepting. It proved to be an impediment of a different kind to full-time work as an historian which I was otherwise happy to have resumed.

A decade or more in the House of Lords and a period as an adviser to the Conservative Party Research Department with a desk at Central Office has certainly been a political education. I now know how different is the feel of an institution if one is associated with its workings from the view that an academic obtains by studying it from the outside. But it has on the whole been too late to make much of such insights in my writing. Unlike many peers, especially those with previous House of Commons experience, I have felt the academic bias sufficiently to fight shy of making speeches on any subject that comes along and have on the whole stuck to areas where I have thought my previous expertise might be of value – constitutional matters, foreign affairs and higher education. Since my views on the last have increasingly

7. I have told this story in my article 'Starting a Private College: A British Experiment in Higher Education', *American Scholar*, XLVIII (3) (Summer 1979).

diverged from those of the government without approximating to those of either opposition party, it has been a controversial and lonely experience.

More germane to the present work was the discovery of the short range of obervation and understanding available to most peers on all sides of the House except for a small handful of other professional historians. History was a subject only dimly thought to be of use to a legislator, and this impression was fortified while watching reactions to the accelerating turmoil in eastern Europe and the Middle East in 1988–91.

But the most controversial episode of my brief political career occurred when I supported the government and the majority of the House of Commons over the War Crimes Bill in 1990–1 against the reiterated opposition of a large proportion of the House of Lords. I had myself taken no part in pressing for such a bill and could see the procedural obstacles in the way of trials for crimes committed outside this country and so long ago. But I felt that, once the bill had come forward, to oppose it was to show a lack of historical understanding of the effect that this might produce not only on the survivors of the Holocaust but on European politics in general. I said at the time and still hold that a barely suppressed anti-Semitism on the part of some of the bill's opponents was obvious from listening to the debate. Once again, the printed word – even Hansard – is inadequate. But for the most part it was the lack of an historical dimension that most impressed me and depressed me. It is not an accident that a denial of the Holocaust itself is a common feature of the neo-Nazi and neo-Fascist movements in the Europe of the 1990s.

Since I do not propose to add to my historical output, the bibliography appended to this volume will show what I have actually produced as a result of this rather unusual exposure to a variety of influences since I published my first book in 1938.[8] By presenting in the chapters that follow a summary of my engagements with history, two further points must be made. In the first place, I could not have chosen a more unpropitious time. Much of what seemed solid ground from which one could look back upon

8.  Max Beloff, *Public Order and Popular Disturbances, 1660–1714* (Oxford: 1938).

the past vanished while I wrote this book in 1990–1. When I began, one had to take the Soviet Union as a fact of life, like the Atlantic Ocean. By the time I completed my task, it no longer existed, nor had anyone any idea of what the consequences of these and other changes – the reunification of Germany for instance – were likely to be. As a schoolboy I could be a Cassandra, but when one approaches the age of eighty prophecy does not become one.[9]

The second point is that in adopting so highly personal an approach to historical writing, I am avoiding the familiar question thrust at the professional historian by philosophers about the degree of objectivity possible for historians. In the United States, the controversies on this issue have been long-standing and bitterly fought, and in 1988 they were the subject of an exhaustive analysis.[10] In the more relaxed atmosphere of British academia, the matter has been less prominent. It has mainly attracted the interest of philosophers with little or no experience of actually writing history. Not since R. G. Collingwood, whose early work *Speculum Mentis* I read as a schoolboy and whose approach has much affected my thinking, have we had a scholar at home equally in the niceties of detailed historical research and academic philosophy. He was one of the giants of my time as a student in Oxford.[11]

On the whole I have followed what I take to be the accepted approach of most of my British contemporaries; one chooses a subject, and then like Foch, 'On s'engage et puis on voit.' And my experience of collaborating with continental as well as American historians suggests that this is equally true for them.[12] After all, one is not going to have the last word, not because one

9.  I can at least claim not to have shared in the common western euphoria about Mikhail Gorbachev. See Max Beloff, 'A Rejoinder to Michael Howard: '1989, a Farewell to Arms?', *International Affairs*, LXV(3) Summer 1989).

10. Peter Novick, *The Noble Dream: The 'Objectivity' Question and the American Historical Profession* (Cambridge: 1988).

11. R. G. Collingwood, *Speculum Mentis* (Oxford: 1924) and *The Idea of History* (Oxford: 1946). For a recent assessment of Collingwood, see Introduction by David Boucher to R. G. Collingwood, *Essays in Political Philosophy* (Oxford: 1989).

12. See Max Beloff, Pierre Renouvin, Franz Schnabel and Franco Valsecchi (eds), *L'Europe du XIX et XX siècle*, 7 vols (Milan: 1959–67).

has failed to be objective, but because the archives (or for ancient historians the digs) are always likely to turn up something new. In my case the shifts in my primary interest from time to time, which I have referred to above and to which I shall return, have made any commitment to a particular school of interpretation rather hard to contemplate. I seem in retrospect never to have been part of any cosy coterie of historians but always to have been something of an outsider.[13] I do not think that the professionalism to which I nevertheless lay claim should inhibit a personal input. Why else write at all? As the painter Caspar David Friedrich wrote: 'The artist should not only paint what he sees before him but also what he sees within him. If however he sees nothing within him, he should desist from painting what he sees before him.' But as my friend the French political theorist Bertrand de Jouvenel once remarked to me: 'You have a very aesthetic approach to these things.'

13. Coteries there have always been, as in other professions and among artists. One did not have to wait for *Past and Present* or 'history workshops'. As an ex-president of the Oxford University Stubbs Society, I am delighted to recall:

> Ladling butter from alternate tubs,
> Stubbs butters Freeman
> Freeman butters Stubbs.

# I

# In Defence of History

In the course of the last century, the study of history has become a major discipline in the universities of the western world, not least in Britain. More recently it has suffered a decline not in the enthusiasm or technical competence of its devotees but in public estimation. It is argued that it lacks direct relevance to contemporary societies and in particular that the rapidity of social change, itself largely the consequence of new technologies, makes the experience of the past of little help in handling the problems it produces, and hence that a grounding in historical knowledge has a smaller place when the young are being prepared for adult life.

Having acquired after retiring from an academic career primarily devoted to historical studies a minor role in public life, I have come up against some of the results of this downgrading of historical studies. One finds among one's Parliamentary colleagues across the political spectrum an unwillingness to face the fact that most of the matters with which government needs to concern itself have roots that stretch back for decades or even centuries. People appear to think that the experience of a few years is enough to guarantee the success of the policies they propound. If our rulers think a knowledge of history unnecessary, why should the ruled think differently?

The damage in respect of domestic affairs may be limited by the degree to which our political leaders have some instinctive relationship to the society from which they have emerged and some feeling for its likely reactions to what they are attempting. But even this may fail if the blinkers of dogma distort or blanket their vision. In respect of foreign affairs, which are increasingly central to our concerns, such instinctive reactions either do not exist or can actually be misleading. In the absence of proper historical knowledge, our expectations of what is going to happen are always likely to be falsified. Events in central and eastern Europe in the watershed years 1989–91 took most people by surprise just as their ancestors were caught unprepared for the consequences of 1789 in France. From a purely practical point of view it is even more worrying that the decline in historical understanding in Britain should be outpaced in the United States, where historical studies have undergone an even more precipitous fall in esteem. Since what the United States does or attempts to do matters more than anything else in the political world, it is more than ever important that the anti-historical bias in American thinking should be corrected.

What then do we need to know? I would put first the require-ment to think in terms of an evolution of society and ideas over very long periods of time. The pace of change does of course vary. It has notably accelerated in the last two centuries. But time itself is a constant. We tend inevitably to telescope the past, so that we feel we can dash in imagination through past centuries as though their years, months and days were somehow shorter and hence less filled with experiences than those of our own era. And this of course is an illusion.

It is even less likely that the accumulation of experience over the centuries does not matter, or that society can choose at any moment to jettison its past and begin afresh. Even when human beings have changed their physical location, as when colonists have migrated to new areas of settlement – and our awareness of the Atlantic migration of the last five centuries should not obscure the fact that migration of one kind and another has been a constant feature of human history – the colonists take in their baggage their languages, their habits, the institutions that permit collective action and their modes of thought. Nor of course do they escape from the constraints of the human condition itself. Whatever conjectures may be made about man's ancestry or prehistorical experience, the human beings we find in our earliest records – and no records, no history – are not all that different from their modern counterparts. The basic human experiences of birth, procreation and death are what they have always been, and so therefore are the possible range of reactions to them. The way in which these reactions are expressed differs in different civiliza-tions and over time. But once we have found the linguistic keys we do not find the art or literature even of the ancient world impenetrable. We may give different interpretations of particular examples but this is equally true when we consider the arts or literature of our own times.

One major change in the human condition has been produced quite recently by developments in medical science. Far more people in the advanced industrial countries reach the psalmist's three score years and ten, or even considerably exceed it. In most parts of the world expectation of life has risen, though there has been a retrogression in some cases, for instance in what was the Soviet Union. But the length of a working life is not significantly longer than it used to be. The experience accumulated is therefore not much more abundant; the handing on of the baton from one generation to the next is not very much delayed. No sudden discontinuities in the human succession parallel the huge changes in such areas as the harnessing of energy, the means of locomotion or the speed of communication.

Such reflections are particularly apposite when we look at what has been since the development of historical writing in the ancient world its main theme, namely the *res publica*. The intimate concerns of the individual human being have been a matter for religious teachers, for philosophers or for the arts. Historians from Herodotus and Thucydides on have dealt with men as members of particular societies, and with the rise and fall of societies and their institutions. War and peace, revolution and counter-revolution, the identification and settlement of political issues – these remain what historians describe and attempt to explain. One can argue about the relative weight that should be given to the role of particular individuals or groups as compared to the underlying and anonymous development of the material and social order. Both approaches have their temptations and their pitfalls, but both are needed and have received equal attention from our major historians in the modern west. Nor have what appear to be instances of pure chance or divine intervention been overlooked. Ultimately the question is how to improve our understanding of why men behaved as they did and what the immediate and long-term consequence of their actions have been.

Arguments from history, real or imaginary, accurate or distorted, have always figured in political debate. Nor are political events without their impact on the writing of history. One immediate result of the loosening of state control in the former Soviet Union since the mid-1980s has been the emergence of a 'revisionist' school of historians trying to bring a new realism into studying the developments that have led to the sufferings its people have endured. A parallel could be drawn with the conflicts among German historians over the different explanations of the rise and fall of the Nazi Reich.

Approaches to political problems have sometimes been influenced by political philosophers, but these writers have contributed relatively little to our actual understanding of human societies. For philosophers who are searching for ways in which to secure their ideals of justice, or equality or freedom or whatever it is they find lacking in the world around them, almost invariably find themselves driven to postulate a different kind of human being starting a new society from scratch. If men were always reasonable and unmoved by passion and prejudice, if they were unacquisitive (or merely acquisitive), if they made no distinction in their feelings between those close to them and more distant members of their societies (to say nothing of other societies) and could therefore ignore the past when creating a new world, then indeed things might be different. But, as the fate of every recorded utopian experiment reminds us, reality is not like that. The musings of political philosophers often bear no more relation to the real world of politics and political economy than science fiction to genuine advances in our mastery of nature.

Nevertheless even if we do not readily accept the view that historical events are moulded by philosophers, that, as has been argued by French historians of the right, the French Revolution was 'caused' by Voltaire and Rousseau, political history must find a place for the ideas that have influenced the minds of men or provided the framework within which they have judged the events of their own times. Nor indeed is it from philosophers that the main assault upon historical studies in the traditional mode now comes.

What is challenged is the view that social development and the political action to which it gives rise form the proper subject of history and that it is to the elucidation of political action that history has the most to contribute. I do not claim that this is a matter of values. Beethoven is certainly more important to me than Napoleon. But just as cultural activity can take place only within a social framework, so the history of culture must accept this fact.

What we are faced with is something different, namely that the whole idea of history as primarily concerned with the development of complete societies and consequently with their institutions, their politics and their conflicts, internal and external, is an error, that we should isolate discrete parts of human activity, each of which has a history of its own, without seeking to fit them in any general framework. The main impetus behind this assault on traditional historiography comes from a variety of sources. One may be described as vaguely anarchist, an expression of the fear that all traditional history becomes nationalist history and a justification of the status quo by an appeal to the past. Analogous to this is what may be regarded as an essentially pacifist approach, the idea that a history of 'kings and battles' is likely to encourage the view that armed conflict has been normal in the past, and that to dwell on it somehow justifies a militaristic attitude to current issues.

Both approaches are largely espoused by educational theorists, who also argue that the interest of children is more likely to be held by dealing with everyday things than with political issues and events which are bound to be remote from their own experience. Such pedagogical arguments can of course be put forward within any society. Others are more precisely related to current politics and to the demand that groups seeking greater recognition today should have their needs attended to by giving more prominence to their role in the past.

In both Britain and the United States two issues of this kind have been to the fore in recent years, one concerning the role of ethnic minorities and the other the role of women. The latter is of course the easier to understand in the double context, since the situation of ethnic groups is so different in the two countries.

The feminist case is in fact doubly flawed, and if accepted would make the writing of history a travesty of the truth unless its whole context were to be redefined. There is no evidence that works of general history either in Britain or in the United States ignore the role of women where their activities impinge upon the political arena. In a country like Britain, where queens regnant have played such an important role, it would be odd if it were otherwise. A history of England that gave little space to Elizabeth I or Queen Victoria would be very peculiar. But until the electoral enfranchisement of women in this century they did not in fact generally play a large role in public affairs except through their influence upon men as wives or mistresses. In the nineteenth century a few exceptionally gifted and determined women did give an impetus to particular social reforms but these instances have never been neglected.

Women have of course played an important part in the economy of all societies, both in their pre-industrial, largely peasant forms and during the subsequent period of industrialization. In general these social facts have been amply considered. But to give a more detailed account of individual contributions is no more possible than with men of similar status. For historical narrative and analysis depend upon the existence of evidence, mainly in the form of written records. Before the advent of mass literacy and the organizations that rely upon it, there is no difference between what can be learned about women and what can be learned about men. We know some medieval monarchs, churchmen, barons and merchants as individuals because their activities have left distinct records or have attracted the attention of contemporary writers. But most other lives can be summarized only statistically, unless by chance some case involving their behaviour has come to the notice of secular or ecclesiastical courts. The moralist can insist on treating peasant and potentate as equals; the historian cannot but differentiate between them because of their differing traces in the record.

In the United States the argument about giving more space to the history of its black population is often equated with the feminist case. But here it is not simply a matter of inadequate sources, it is also the fact that for most of the country's history its black inhabitants, first as slaves and latterly subject to varying forms of discrimination, were more the objects of policy than active participants in its formulation. Historians of the United States, with no kings and fewer battles to chronicle, have quite reasonably found their guiding thread in the development of their unique constitutional system. But this system was established by a generation in which political activity was wholly confined to white males of the propertied class and of Anglo-Saxon origin. Had George Washington been a black woman, historians would have recorded the fact. But he was not. Today of course both women and blacks play important parts in that country's political and judicial institutions, but it would be misleading if this were thought to demand that the absence of their participation in the past should somehow be glossed over.

A rather different problem may now be arising in the United States as a result of recent immigration from Latin American countries and some Asian countries. These newcomers may seek not integration but some form of multiculturalism, as has come to be true of a minority of blacks. In this respect there may be a greater similarity with Britain, where most of the ethnic minorities are of relatively recent provenance. Is the teaching of history of Britain to give weight to this presence and if so how? The issue has been coming to the fore with arguments over the historical content of the national curriculum. Ought the offspring of recent immigrants be taught conventional British history, including the long periods during which their ancestors were not present on the British scene, so as to give them the maximum understanding of the society in which they will be seeking their fortunes, or should they study instead the history of the countries from which their families originate?[1]

In the British case there is the particular twist given by the presence in the new ethnic communities of militant Islam, which makes many specific educational demands. But of course wherever there are important religious differences history becomes harder to teach. For those whose heritage is Christian, the word 'crusade' is a 'hurrah word' (in the terminology of logical positivists), while for Moslems and for Jews it is a 'boo word'. Protestant and Catholic historians will not look in quite the same way on Elizabeth I or William III.

Whatever compromises are reached on such issues, it is clear that they do not provide a reason for depriving the majority community of its desirable immersion in its own history or of pride in the nation's achievements. Otherwise a healthy patriotism is likely to be replaced by an unhealthy nationalism with racist overtones.

We have not so far encountered in Britain that extreme of sentiment which has persuaded American universities to demote the history of western civilization and the study of western intellectual and artistic heritage from its proper place in undergraduate education. Such pressures have found American universities, which have never shown much conviction in academic self-defence, all too willing to concede the claims – claims advanced not on the whole by representatives of the allegedly injured

---

1.  I have tried briefly to explain the particular nature of the British problem in this respect to American readers in my article 'The British Debate on the Teaching of History', *Continuity*, 14 (Spring/Fall 1990). The American problem is fully explored in Dinesh D'Souza, *Illiberal Education: The Politics of Race and Sex on Campus* (New York: 1991). The author himself is an Indian immigrant into the United States.

minorities but by exponents of radical chic anxious to show their sensitivity to the possibilities of giving offence.

Problems of this kind are not unique to Britain or the United States. In this cruel twentieth century, we must presume that migrations will continue and diasporas survive. People belonging to one cultural tradition but living in a society with a different one have the difficult task of relating their sense of history to more than one world. In rare cases this can be a stimulus; for many it will be a burden.

The unreality of some of the fashionable criticism of traditional history should not lead one to overlook its actual shortcomings. Our minds have largely been conditioned by our own upbringing within the confines of western civilization, however defined and demarcated. Our linguistic capabilities may also tend to focus our attention on the near rather than the far. Yet it would be absurd to claim that western history is the only history, or that the rest of the world can be dismissed as only a stage for the expansion of the west and its ideas. If one deals only with very recent centuries, a case can indeed be made that the main impulse for change has been that expansion and its repercussions. But as we go backwards in time we are confronted with the wholly or almost wholly self-contained development of other civilizations – Chinese, Japanese, Hindu, Islamic, Aztec, Inca. Since there is no reason to believe that the impact upon our world by those who survive has been nullified by the recent primacy of the west, the study of them is germane to our current concerns. But to put this perception fully into effect is something beyond the range of even the most devoted scholar. Philosophers of history prepared to use the work of others as building blocks in their own constructions – Spengler, Toynbee – may give due place to non-western experience.[2] But such a synoptic vision is given to few.[3]

If one has no such vision one must do the best one can with the history one has learned and accept one's limitations. As I explained in the Introduction, I began as an historian of seventeenth-century Britain. And I have retained from that early

2.  Arnold J. Toynbee's A *Study of History* appeared in twelve volumes between 1934 and 1961. For an account of its genesis and composition see William H. McNeill, *Arnold J. Toynbee: A Life* (Oxford: 1989) and my review of this biography in *Encounter* (April 1990).
3.  See for instance, on the Second World War, Christopher Thorne, *The Issues of War: States, Societies and the Far Eastern Conflict* (London: 1985).

interest an abiding one in the constitutional and political arrangements of the British state.

Many of the constitutional issues were raised and some settled during the seventeenth century. That century's history consequently attracted foreign admirers of British Parliamentary institutions. A former member of the Second Duma in Russia, Jacob Schapiro, one of the few Jews among its members, who sat for what had historically been called Dorpat but had been renamed Yuriev by the Russians and is now Tartu in Latvia, sought exile in this country after the dissolution of the Duma and set about collecting printed original sources and major secondary works relating to that period. Through my family's friendship with Jacob Schapiro, I eventually acquired this collection, which gave an impetus to my choice of a field of specialization. I was told that my best marks in my final Schools in Oxford were in the special subject Commonwealth and Protectorate.

My own interest in British constitutional questions was to shift forward in time, as was appropriate for a professor of Government and Public Administration. But I never abandoned it and found such questions once again of direct relevance to aspects of the work of the House of Lords in the last decade. It was perhaps knowing about these English seventeenth-century developments (which did not affect Scotland in the same way), as well as something of the Russian constitutional movement before 1917, that made me a defender of the independence of the bar in the battle over legal 'reforms' in 1989.

Second in my interests has always been the history of France – at first awakened by Alexandre Dumas and later by other French novelists, but no doubt directed by reading French history as presented both by France's own historians and by a number of English scholars who have devoted themselves to the affairs of our closest and most challenging neighbour, my teacher Denis Brogan among them. I have written almost nothing on the subject but it must rank high when looking at Britain's relations with continental Europe, which have been a preoccupation of mine for so many years.

Accident dictated my other two major historical ventures, which proved to overlap – one arose from my being the only person available in a war-depleted university history department to teach American history when the entry of the United States into the war made its omission from the university curricula a matter of some embarrassment. It may well be that my approach was idiosyncratic, since unlike most British scholars who have subsequently contributed to this subject I did not have the experience of proper training in an American graduate school. My own library on this subject (now at the University of Buckingham) was built up with as little guidance as my own lectures. My previous concern with British constitutional argument no doubt affected the priority I gave to the constitutional aspects of the great turning points in history of the United States and would be fairly unfashionable today.

While I was still engaged in filling the gaps in my knowledge of American history I was as already noted, asked by Chatham House to take up the study of Soviet foreign policy as part of its preparatory work for the problems of the post-war period. I spent some six years working in the Soviet field, but I was not tempted to remain in it: too much hidden, too little available of interest to someone trying for more than a mere chronicle. And for a number of years the situation was to remain much the same. My book remained a standard textbook in Britain and the USA for much longer than would have been the case if I had been dealing with a less enclosed and secretive country than Stalin's Russia.[4] Now, of course, things have changed. More material is being released and Soviet historians themselves, no longer inhibited by having to attribute infallibility to Stalin, are busy with revisionism. We are also witnessing an enormous growth of such studies in the west as people plunge further back into both Soviet and pre-Soviet Russian history to elucidate the changes that have been taking place.

So it was back to British, American and general European history. The work I did on European history with my continental colleagues was influenced by the growing interest in the possibilities of a new pan-European concern looking at ways in which conflict had come about to see how it might be avoided. In so far as it involved drawing lessons from the inter-war period, I tended to take rather different views from those then current among many British and American historians. They had looked at such issues as 'collective security' and 'appeasement' from the point of view of relations between Germany and her western neighbours. I, having come to this study via my reading of Soviet policy, took a different stance.

4.   Max Beloff, *The Foreign Policy of Soviet Russia, 1929–1941*, 2 vols (Oxford: 1947 and 1949).

The main driving force in European studies after the war was, however, forward- rather than backward-looking. It was a question of what new institutions might be founded to embody the new drive for unity.[5] And this in turn raised the question, which is still with us, of the precise relationship of Britain to such developments; is Britain another European country which happens to be an island or is it bound to remain semi-detached?[6]

Curiously enough it was the debate over Britain and Europe that launched me into my final venture into serious historical research, a study of Britain's imperial decline.[7] Here again this had repercussions on my understanding of the inter-war years. If the Commonwealth was indeed the reason for Britain's holding back from the moves towards European unity in the 1950s and 1960s, what had been the earlier impact on British policy of a concentration on imperial responsibilities? It was also a revelation of what I have already referred to, the need to understand other civilizations in their own right if the imperial experience is to be properly understood. Nor, if I could now return to Russian interests, would the study of how the British Empire came to an end fail to indicate questions about the crisis through which the Soviet Empire – the last European empire – has passed. But not all imperial powers are or have been European. China presents one problem that could hardly be ignored, if only from a sense of its size, its population and the continuity of its independent history. Yet what historian of Europe can also hope to be a competent sinologist?

The same difficulties of interpretation clearly confront those seeking to understand Japan. Here there is an element of additional paradox since modern technology and the industrial and financial base it has created seem to give Japan an air of modernity. Yet its political and social institutions and habits and

5. Typical of the period and its mood is the report I wrote for a study group set up by the Council of Europe: Max Beloff, *Europe and the Europeans* (London: 1957). It is notable that this book appeared also in German, Italian, Spanish and Portuguese, and perhaps equally notable that it did not appear in French.

6. I had occasion to return to this theme when writing a paper on 'Churchill and Europe' for a conference on 'Winston S. Churchill' at the University of Texas, Austin in March 1991.

7. Max Beloff, *Imperial Sunset*, vol. 1: *Britain's Liberal Empire, 1897–1921* (London: 1969; New York: 1970. 2nd edn, London: 1987; New York: 1988), vol. 2: *Dream of Commonwealth, 1921–1942* (London: 1989; New York: 1989).

its cultural disposition make it hard either to sustain a fully meaningful dialogue or to forecast its future evolution.

Whether the Hispanic and Lusitanian countries of the New World are also destined to figure more prominently in the international arena, who can say? Ignorant of the two languages and all but the barest outlines of Spanish and Portuguese history, it would be arrogant for me to venture into Latin American history. Yet how can someone interested in empire overlook Spain's successes and failures, both in Europe and in the Americas?[8] The only point I would make at this stage of the argument is to question the misleading habit of grouping the Latin American republics with countries in Asia and Africa to form the so-called Third World. Definitions based wholly on negative attributes are rarely useful.

Equally, as a sometime historian of the British Empire, I am aware how distinct are the personalities of the lands in Asia and Africa, the Caribbean and the Pacific that made it up. I do not believe that such countries can be approached with any confidence that their feelings, motives and designs are easily penetrable from outside. Where mutual comprehension is concerned, it may be easier for Indians – to take the country that matters most – than for the British to get it right. I owe much to Nirad Chaudhuri, but his capacities for empathy far exceed mine.[9] Again generations of Englishmen have prided themselves on their good understanding of, and their good understanding with, Arabs and Iranians, but recent developments in the Islamic world suggest that they were over-optimistic on both counts. If history is to be a practical guide to what we must do about that part of the world, we have yet to discover how to use it.

In some cases it may be that the peoples themselves at least know where they stand and what they desire, even if their reasoning is couched in a different mode from our own. With Africans, whether emerging from colonial rule on their own continent or mediated through generations of slavery in the New World, the case is more complex, because their own self-image has changed more than once since emanicipation and the ending

8.  See for instance, Anthony Pagden, *Spanish Imperialism and the Political Imagination* (New Haven and London: 1990).
9.  Nirad Chaudhuri, *The Autobiography of an Unknown Indian* (London: 1951), and also *Thy Hand Great Anarch! India, 1921–1952* (London: 1987).

of external rule. Western statesmen, brought up in the belief that to every problem there is a rational solution which men of goodwill sitting down together can always discover, find it hard to accept that some gulfs are unbridgeable. Historians have no such commitment.

Both the creation of new institutions for Europe and the demise of empires raise questions about the nature and origin of the building blocks of history – nations. Much has been written on nations and nationalism, and the literature is added to whenever a new upheaval raises particular questions about their status and rights.[10] The historian of Europe is bound to be influenced by the history of the two countries in which for two centuries the national question has been to the fore and which by example and action have had a major impact in central, eastern and south-eastern Europe – Italy and Germany. On neither have I done any serious work nor will this volume deal with them specifically.

In the case of Italy the influence it has exerted as a cultural and (though not until quite late) a political entity makes its very being a part of Britain's and indeed of all Europe's history from the Renaissance onwards.[11] In the case of Germany, I feel the in-evitable inhibitions of any Jew. It is so hard not to see German history moving towards the unimaginable horror of the Holocaust. And while seeing no reason at all to burden a new generation with the sins of their fathers and grandfathers, and while freely admitting that the Nazi episode was a brief interlude in Germany's often rich and creative history, it is difficult to be certain that one is not affected in one's interpretation of the remoter past by frightening echoes of yesterday.[12]

Almost every time one approaches the history of any European nation, the same ambiguities appear. How long has it been a nation? Is what we refer to today the same nation as in the past?

10.   For a brief attempt to encapsulate the European problem for American readers see my essay 'Fault Lines and Steeples: The Divided Loyalties of Europe', *National Interest*, 23 (Spring 1991).

11.   My contacts with Italian historians were sufficient for me to be invited to an historical conference in Rome in 1970 to celebrate the centenary of the acquisition of Rome by the kingdom of Italy. Max Beloff, 'Il problema di Roma nella politica della Gran Bretagna', in *Atti del XLV Congresso di Storia del Risorgimento Italiano* (Rome: 1972).

12.   I have found much illumination on the problem of Germany's acquisition of national political self-consciousness in James J. Sheehan, *German History, 1770–1866* (Oxford: 1990).

Poland, which has shifted its geographical location more than once and yet has a recognizable and individual history both in its long conjunction with Lithuania and on its own, is an obvious case in point. [13]

With Poland as with Germany, as earlier with Spain, much of the history of the Jewish diaspora is embedded in their national histories. Once again, Jewish history is not an area in which I can claim professional training. Apart from what I may have acquired over the years by osmosis as it were, I am mainly indebted to intermittent reading stimulated by the emergence of the State of Israel and by the contacts I have enjoyed with Israeli historians, some of them my pupils. But, while the antecedents of Zionism are to be found in the history of the diaspora, Israel is not wholly a product of Europe nor is it situated within its conventional boundaries. Its destiny is bound up with what we have learned to call the Middle East; not only Jerusalem but also Cairo, Damascus and Baghdad figure in its birth and survival.

The paradox of a national identity within a common cultural framework has been one that has intrigued me ever since I was an undergraduate, perhaps because of the example provided by music, which I regarded as the west's major achievement. Alone of the arts, it transcends the barriers of time but not of space. Western music has a single origin and for centuries composers and performers – originally often the same persons – have crossed and recrossed political frontiers. Yet the three great strands in nineteenth-century music – Italian, German, Russian – have an unmistakable national imprint. And England and France, with their less formidable musical output, have national characteristics apparent to the listener, if not easily defined. In recent years, one has also been struck by the fact that whereas western music has made little impact in Africa or South Asia (indeed, rather the reverse), the Japanese and to a lesser extent the Chinese and Koreans have produced interpreters of western music, particularly where string instruments are concerned, who, within a certain range, are second to none. What does Mozart mean to a Japanese? Japan did not participate in the Enlightenment. There are puzzles here.

So far I have been writing of the major themes with which modern historians deal – the rise and fall of states and empires,

13.  The subject is treated effectively and imaginatively in Adam Zamoyski, *The Polish Way* (London: 1987).

the governance of men – and have argued that, despite my admiration for the French social historians of the *Annales* school, in the end one comes back to political action and the actual behaviour of individuals in their political setting.[14] But, for this concentration to be successful, broad generalities are not sufficient. One must be aware all the time of the possibly deceptive nature of appearances and of the way in which things take on a different aspect when one approaches them more closely.

The skills of the miniaturist are as essential to the historian as the skills of a painter on larger canvases. At some point every apprentice to the historical profession must learn what happens when one immerses oneself in original documents. There is no other way of discovering how decisions are actually arrived at, even though for all but a tiny proportion of what one may wish to discuss one has to rely upon the work of others. Even my own minor involvement in party politics over the last decade has made me more aware of the difficulty for those not involved in the action of getting at the truth. 'Open government', so much talked about nowadays, is a contradiction in terms.

What is true of the present is equally true of the past. The picture of events presented to the public is not and cannot be the whole truth; even if there is nothing particularly discreditable to hide, the characters in the story are rarely as single-minded as they or their biographers would have us believe.

Many years ago, when my historical interests were still being formed, I read Disraeli's *Life of Lord George Bentinck*. It was written soon after the repeal of the Corn Laws and the fall of Peel. Disraeli, with his talent as a novelist as well as the advantage of an intimate involvement in the events described, gave a splendid and compelling account. Now with the publication of his letters for these years we can see that in his daily round other things bulked equally large: his precarious finances, his complicated relations with his wife and sister, his advancement in society in London and Paris, his obligations to his publishers, his worries about his own Parliamentary seat. How did Peel and the Corn Laws fit in?[15] Gladstone's diaries have similarly added important nuances to our standard picture of the 'People's William'.

14. I believe I was the first British historian to call attention to Fernand Braudel's epoch-making book – on the old Third Programme of the BBC: Fernand Braudel, *La Méditerranée et le monde méditerranéan a l'époque de Philippe II* (Paris: 1949).
15. *Benjamin Disraeli Letters*, vol. iv: *1842–1847* (Toronto: 1989).

In an age when correspondence takes a much smaller place in people's lives and in politics, and when those who write letters and receive them rarely have the house room in which to preserve them, we may feel that future historians will be much worse off than those concerned with the public figures of the nineteenth century or even of the eighteenth. Nor is 'oral history' a satisfactory substitute, since it relies on memory, and no one's memory can be trusted.[16]

In what follows in the present volume I shall be shifting my ground from time to time from the general to the particular and back. But about the 'truth' I remain a sceptic. Sometimes I think the novelist may be a better guide to what we need to know and understand. Trollope's political novels are worth innumerable academic theses about nineteenth-century politics; Paul Scott's *Raj Quartet* is more illuminating than anything else that has been written about the 'transfer of power' in India. Historians do a more mundane job and are perhaps rightly less well regarded and less well rewarded.

16.    One of the greatest pleasures that research ever gave me was the discovery, when working on the project for an Anglo-French Union during the crisis of 1940, that the accounts in print of all the principal participants could be shown to be factually inaccurate. Max Beloff, 'The Anglo-French Union Project of 1940', reprinted from *Mélanges: Pierre Renouvin* (Paris: 1966) in Max Beloff, *The Intellectual in Politics and Other Essays* (London: 1970). An earlier pleasurable discovery made while working on my B. Litt. Thesis was that Sidney and Beatrice Webb had begun their histories of British local government under the quite mistaken impression that the Glorious Revolution marked an important shift in responsibilities in this area. It was also a salutary warning.

# II

## *The Uniqueness of Britain*

After much argument there seems to be a general acceptance of the view embodied in the national curriculum that British history should have a distinctive role in the education of children in British schools whatever their ethnic background or religious (or non-religious) affiliation. But the definition of British history itself presents us with problems that go beyond those of the school curriculum. What do we mean by British? It has been powerfully argued that if such a thing as British history exists then it must not be just English history but must take into account all the peoples who live or have lived in what can be described as an Atlantic offshore archipelago.[1] The interaction of these peoples – English, Scots, Welsh and Irish – has been the setting of many of the main events in British history, and the conflicts to which it has given rise are by no means exhausted. Each of these peoples has its own version and myths of this British past.[2]

In addition, while the narrow seas have to some extent permitted British separateness from developments on the neighbouring continent, invasion by Romans (before the English came) and the Danes and Normans afterwards have all played their part

1. See J. G. A. Pocock, 'British History: A Plea for a New Subject', *Journal of Modern History*, XLVII (1975); 'The Limits and Divisions of British History: In Search of an Unknown Subject', *American Historical Review*, LXXXVII (1982).
2. In his inaugural lecture at University College London in January 1991, Professor Conrad Russell emphasized the importance of taking the other British realms into account when explaining the course of the seventeenth-century revolution and Civil War.

in fashioning British civilization.[3] So too have other immigrant groups seeking refuge or fortune in these islands, of whom the ethnic minorities of today are only the latest examples.

Against this argument for using the word 'British' must be set the fact that it has been, in the last resort, English institutions and ways of doing that that have triumphed, except finally in what is now the Irish Republic. The circumstances in which the component parts of the United Kingdom came together, and the balance established between its component peoples were different in each case. But, during the period of Britain's major impact on the world through imperial expansion and world-wide commerce, all the peoples of the islands participated in a venture of which the directing forces were the City of London and the Parliament at Westminster. And this was true of the military as well as the civil aspects of these achievements.

It may be the case that this apparent dominance of the English aspect of the story owes something to the better preservation of records of the English state – both Scottish and Irish records have suffered much destruction. As has been said, 'the guardianship of one's past is power; the court of record is the kernel of English government'.[4] Indeed the importance attached by the Scots at the time of the Union and ever since to keeping their own legal system as well as their own ecclesiastical establishment may be held to support this thesis. The Irish and the Welsh have relied more upon cultural distinctiveness as the key to their separate identities.[5]

If what is distinctive about Britain is the continuity of its institutions, monarchy, courts, Parliament, it is the English elements that provide it. In that sense when we say British history we often mean English history.[6]

3. I owe my introduction to this theme to a now forgotten book, Esmé Wingfield Stratford, *The History of British Civilization*, published in 1928 (2nd edn, London: 1930), which I received as a school prize (for geography) in 1930.
4. Pocock, 'British History', p. 601.
5. On Ireland see R. E. Foster, *Modern Ireland, 1600–1972* (London: 1988). Arthur Griffith, who had fought for the Boers and was to play an important part in the events of 1918–22, argued in his book published in 1904, *The Resurrection of Hungary: A Parallel for Ireland*, that an Ireland given equal constitutional status with England could be a partner in running the British Empire.
6. The historian of imperial expansion, Sir John Seeley, was ambiguous on this issue, calling his major work published in 1893 *The Expansion of England*,

English history was indeed the core of what was taught in schools and universities when modern history became part of a liberal education. The argument for this pre-eminence was derived from a stress upon the importance of continuity. Furthermore there was at the time much visual evidence for that continuity. To an even greater degree than in other western European countries where mountains and forests survive, the English landscape is man-made. And relative internal peace meant the survival of more buildings.

We have had, particularly recently, many historians who have examined and are examining this physical heritage, and its existence has always been implicit in English historical writing, though no one has treated the idea in the masterly fashion in which Fernand Braudel handled the French parallel.[7] We follow roads that go back to the Roman occupation, though until relatively recently we had no idea what a wealth of Roman remains might still be uncovered.[8] We have parish churches and cathedrals that have welcomed worshippers since the Middle Ages and cities that in their street plans and their buildings give direct visual access to the past. Alone in Europe we have ancient collegiate universities where undergraduates can converse on issues of current politics in rooms where the Armada, the Restoration or Napoleon might have been discussed.

On the other hand both the rural and urban landscape have suffered major changes in the last half-century. Much of the countryside has been engulfed by the spread of suburbia, and its typical aspects destroyed by new forms of mechanized agriculture and by the further deforestation (and afforestation) that has taken place. Town centres partly destroyed by the Luftwaffe and subsequently by urban 'planners' make their historical antecedents difficult to visualize. Where is Wren's London skyline that Wordsworth admired and the Prince of Wales mourns? It is true that more historic houses are open to the public and that there are more museums with more ingenuity going into them. But, in

while his last work published posthumously was entitled *The Growth of British policy*. See Deborah Wormell, *Sir John Seeley and the Uses of History* (Cambridge: 1980).

7.   Fernand Braudel, *L'Identité de la France*, 3 vols (Paris: 1986).
8.   The volume on Roman Britain in *The Oxford History of England*, *Roman Britain and the English Settlements* by R. G. Collingwood and J. N. L. Myres was replaced by a new volume by Peter Salway, *Roman Britain* (Oxford: 1981).

seeking these and other monuments, tourists help to vitiate by their very presence and by what is contrived to meet their physical needs precisely the atmosphere that they hoped to find in the first place. It is becoming increasingly hard to visualize what England looked and sounded like before the motor-car. The most obvious feature of historic England was the great local variety crammed into an area less than that of most American states. But it is now giving way to a homogenization that used to be thought typical of America itself. Even if we confine ourselves to England, the historian's task is greater than it was.

It is certainly the case that it is England not Britain that has attracted foreign observers, despite the Auld Alliance between Scotland and France. For three centuries, foreigners have sought the explanation in constitutional terms of England's apparent capacity to assimilate without succumbing to authoritarianism or to revolutionary violence the accelerating processes of social change. In particular, French liberals from Voltaire and Montesquieu to Tocqueville and Prévost Paradol have tried to find English institutions they could commend to their compatriots.[9] Nor, as I have already pointed out, did this interest confine itself to France or indeed to western Europe. There seemed nothing incongruous in seeking lessons for the reform of Tsarism in the English seventeenth century. And it seemed perfectly in order for the parents of a promising boy in the Bukovina (at that time, 1925, in Romania) to send him to university in England, because of their enormous regard for Britain's social and political system and cultural climate.[10] While Britain's power and prestige do not stand where they then did, the upheavals in eastern Europe in 1989–9 again sent parliamentarians and would-be parliamentarians to England to see how our system worked.

The emulation of British institutions was encouraged by British statesmen themselves, particularly in the Victorian heyday. Palmerston's tendency to equate the spread of liberal institutions,

9.  See my chapter 'The Impact of the French Revolution upon British Statecraft, 1789–1921' in Ceri Crossley and Ian Small (eds), *The French Revolution and British Culture* (Oxford: 1989).
10. Eric Roll (Lord Roll), *Crowded Hours* (London: 1985). He goes on to recall conversations between his parents and a deputy in the Romanian Parliament when the fate of the Bukovina seemed still unsettled 'in which they all agreed that the ideal solution would be that it should become a British colony'.

even when in a nationalist garb, with British interests was under-standable. Liberal societies seemed more likely to provide the conditions in which trade could flourish and British businessmen travel freely in pursuit of profit. It was therefore possible for him to say without incurring the charge of hypocrisy that 'the real policy of England – apart from questions which involve her own particular interests, political or commercial – is to be the champion of justice and right – pursuing that course with modera-tion and prudence not becoming the Quixote of the world' and to echo Canning in saying that 'the interests of England ought to be the shibboleth of policy'.[11] It is understandable that at any given time the leading industrial nation should favour open societies and non-discrimination in commerce; in that sense American policy in the last sixty years has been as obvious as was Britain's in Palmerston's day.

In some respects, Gladstone three decades later expounded the same principle that in British foreign policy there should be 'a sympathy with freedom, a desire to give it scope, founded not upon visionary ideas but upon the long experience of many generations within the shores of this happy isle, that in freedom you lay the firmest foundations both of loyalty and order'.[12] Yet Gladstone's, view was based not simply on consideration of British interest but also upon a sympathy on religious and humanitarian grounds with oppressed peoples, particularly those Christian peoples subject to the tyrannical rule of the Turks – the same sympathy that had motivated Byron and the other philhellenes of the 1820s.[13] In this respect, Disraeli's cautious approach to the contest for the Balkans was more in keeping with a pragmatic concern for British material interests.[14]

It was not only those entrusted with office who felt able in the light of Britain's power and influence to take up the cause of oppressed nationalities. In a country which gave free asylum to political refugees from many quarters, there would be no lack of individuals and publications to keep before the public instances of oppression abroad. The adoption of some national group in

11. Viscount Palmerston, speech in the House of Commons, 1 March 1848.
12. W. E. Gladstone, speech at West Calder, Midlothian, 27 November 1879.
13. William St Clair, *That Greece Might Still Be Free: The Philhellenes and the War of Independence* (London: 1972).
14. On Gladstone's anti-Turkish campaign see R. W. Seton-Watson, *Disraeli, Gladstone and the Eastern Question* (London: 1935).

eastern or south-eastern Europe or in Turkey – in Asia – by a British public figure or, latterly, a journalist was a testimony to national self-confidence.

Sometimes this interest in foreign persecutions was more or less fortuitous. Occasionally there might be a specific reason. For instance, the Jewish community had a special interest in objecting to the increasing closeness of ties with Russia as British foreign policy came to be dominated by the German challenge after the turn of the century.[15] In the diplomacy of war and of the peace-making that followed between 1919 and 1922, such dedicated protagonists of one side or another in the European conflicts of the time had opportunities to influence statesmen and diplomats and even to take an active part in the affairs of the would-be governments of the new or enlarged states.

The career in this respect of the historian R. W. Seton-Watson is particularly illuminating.[16] He began earlier in the century by espousing the cause of the Hungarians, popular in England since the revolutions of 1848. But closer acquaintance made him aware that the *Ausgleich* with Austria had turned the Hungarians from being victims to being in a sense joint oppressors of the non-German, non-Magyar elements in the Habsburg Empire. He thus took up the cause of the Czechs, and of the Slovaks, the Romanians and the southern Slavs.[17] Greeks, Bulgarians and Albanians found other champions while the Magyars, the main losers territorially in 1919, found a defender in Aylmer Macartney.[18]

Linking Europe with the Middle East was the Zionist move-ment, also championed by British statesmen, scholars and journal-ists for a variety of reasons, in which the religious and the material are sometimes hard to separate. Equally powerful during the war and afterwards was the pressure of the Arabophiles, personified by

15.  See Max Beloff, 'Lucien Wolf and the Anglo-Russian Entente, 1907–1914', in *The Intellectual in Politics and Other Essays.* (London: 1970).
16.  Hugh Seton-Watson and Christopher Seton-Watson, *The Making of the New Europe: R. W. Seton-Watson and the Last Years of Austro-Hungary* (London: 1981).
17.  C. Boden and Hugh Seton-Watson (eds), *R. W. Seton-Watson and the Romanians* (Bucharest, 1988); Hugh Seton-Watson and Christopher Seton-Watson (eds), *R. W. Seton-Watson and the Yugoslavs: Correspondence, 1906–1941* (London and Zagreb: 1976).
18.  See Hugh Seton-Watson, 'Carlile Aylmer Macartney, 1895–1978', *Proceedings of the British Academy*, LXVII (1981).

T. E. Lawrence, who imbued the relationship with romance. What links all these various manifestations of the emotional involvement of Britons with other peoples is the belief that they could be brought to accept the validity of British-style constitutionalism, an illusion similar to that which was to endow emergent African states with the 'Westminster model' during the period of 'decolonization'.[19]

In stressing the importance of Britain's political institutions, and especially of Parliament, foreigners have thus only echoed a particular aspect of Britain's own self-regard. This element in the British outlook became even more pronounced with the break in constitutional continuity which was the consequence in other countries of the Nazi and Soviet conquests. The importance attached in Britain to Parliament has been an important element in the British opposition to absorption in a European political union, an idea which has been so attractive elsewhere in western Europe. Other countries may not be behind Britain in their determination to forward and secure their national interests but they do not identify their national identity with their legislatures.

In all this there is of course an element of illusion. Parliament today does not much resemble that described by Bagehot; still less does it resemble the Parliament that fought Charles I or that was the instrument through which Henry VIII secured the break with Rome, and that Parliament too would have been unrecognizable to Simon de Montfort. On the other hand, there is a genuine contrast between countries that also had proto-parliaments in the Middle Ages in the shape of gatherings of Estates but lost them during the period of monarchical absolutism from the sixteenth century on, and Britain, in which Parliamentary institutions though at times threatened by the same forces survived and triumphed.

The argument for the Parliamentary tradition being genuine is more acceptable than that for the unbroken persistence of the idea of constitutional monarchy. For here Britain was touched in the middle of the nineteenth century by fashionable republicanism and it took a considerable effort, and a quite self-conscious one, from the last years of Victoria's reign to the present day to give

19. Difficult to explain in these terms is Arnold Toynbee's espousal of the Turkish cause against the Greeks during their conflict after the First World War. See William H. McNeil, *Arnold J. Toynbee: A Life* (Oxford: 1989).

the monarchy its current role as the national symbol and as a focus for unity in a country deephy divided by party strife.[20]

The question is a particularly British one, and not one to which contemporary historians give clear and unequivocal answers. This would not have been the case to the same extent a generation or two ago; and it must be remembered that the opinions of practical men are most likely to have been formed by the residue of what they have learned or half-learned earlier on. Foreigners also are little likely to be affected by the latest trends in the historical scholarship in another country.

Much of the impetus to revisionism arises from the mere expansion of the historians' profession, which is itself the consequence, here as in other countries, of the growth in size and number of institutions of higher education. Young people seeking to get their foot on the academic ladder in history as in any other disciplines must show their capacities for research. While some topics for these arise from the overall view and requirements of the young researcher's supervisor or patron, as in the German classical model, it is probable that more attention will be paid to his work if it is of a kind to challenge accepted notions.[21] Of course this is not to say that scholars may not find themselves revising accepted views because they have found a body of material that causes them to question what they have been taught about a particular problem or period. In their treatment of historical themes they are also likely to be increasingly affected by ideas and techniques developed in the social sciences, economics, anthropology, demography, sociology and even linguistics.

Anyone surveying, however superficially, the output of British historians today finds himself confronted over and over again with sharply contrasting views on the relation between social and political change. To some extent this has always been the case.

20. For some reflections on the making of the modern monarchy by its servants see the essays under the heading 'Royalty' in David Cannadine, *The Pleasures of the Past* (London: 1989).

21. When I was an aspiring research student I went to see the late Sir George Clark. He, as was his custom, fished in his drawer for the list of possible seventeenth-century topics and allowed me to choose. I was promised if successful a footnote in the second edition of his volume on *The Later Stuarts* in *The Oxford History of England*. I was, as I have already noticed, embarked upon another of Clark's suggestions when I was swept into new fields of study by wartime demands. Not all historians of course are as respectful of the learning of their elders as I have been.

Since people's own religious and political views both derive from and affect their picture of the relevant past, one would expect differences of opinion and emphasis over the Reformation, the Civil War, the Glorious Revolution and so on. In the nineteenth century, however, the tendency to see the past in terms of the emergence of the rule of law and of Parliamentary institutions as giving the country's history a particular twist was clearly uppermost. So too has been the more recent tendency to see a turning point earlier in this century in the development and expansion of a 'welfare state', though here the distinctiveness of Britain's experience from that of her neighbours is much less striking. All modern industrial societies have in one form or another seen a growth in state intervention, even if through different techniques.

It is of course disturbing to be told how much of British history requires revision or how the different lines of research produce different answers. Was the Civil War precipitated by the demands of a rising class of gentry or by the reaction to a decline in their revenues and status? Was the Glorious Revolution a landmark in the history of British liberties or simply the culmination of a plot between a foreign prince and native malcontents?[22] Did the industrial revolution raise or lower the living standards of the working classes? Was the British Empire a major force for spreading material progress and good government or merely a vehicle for the greed of individual capitalists? Was Britain in any way responsible for either of the two world wars which have been so fateful for her own story?

Many of these and similar questions reproduce debates current in the period referred to; others are the product of asking new questions. Alan Macfarlane for instance, by investigating English medieval property rights, has arguably pushed back by centuries the point at which England does not conform to our basic understanding of European feudalism, so that the industrial revolution and all that goes with it are seen as fortifying not inaugurating the

---

22. It is a testimony to the extreme sensitivity of Britain's current rulers to minority attitudes that, when the Glorious Revolution fell to be celebrated in 1988, the fortification of British liberties against a continental-style Roman Catholic absolutism was pushed into the background and the accent in the official exhibition and accompanying ceremonies was placed on the relatively minor and transitory link with the Dutch House of Orange.

specifically English attitude to individual rights and to the role of the state.[23] Again one has to take into account what might seem an opposite train of thought in the work of a young historian, Jonathan Clark, who suggests that seventeenth- and eighteenth-century England were also part of the *ancien régime*, that religion remained a key to political allegiances and that Jacobitism was a real menace to the Revolution settlement for long afterwards and not merely a nostalgic set of outmoded loyalties.[24]

My own contribution to the Edward Arnold *New History of England* was treated by some reviewers as an example of historical revisionism, if of a reactionary kind, in its neglect of changes in social habits and in its lack of obeisance to the welfare-state consensus. It was even described as 'Thatcherite' history, although I personally have found free-market dogmatism as hard to swallow as its socialist or Keynesian rivals.[25]

In a period of such uncertainty about the British past and of such political tensions as Britain struggles towards an appropriate role in a new Europe and a new distribution of world power and influence, it is not surprising that there should be on the part of rulers and would-be rulers some resistance to basing prescriptions for policy on past experience. Appeals to the past, whether from a radical though nominally Conservative government or from its socialist and Liberal Democrat opponents, have been equally selective in their choice and interpretation of events. In seeking to reform the British legal system in 1989–90, the Lord Chancellor of the day – himself a product of the Scottish Roman-law-based system – proved deaf to all arguments that rested upon the beliefs that it has been the existence of an independent bar and an independent system of courts in close symbiosis with it that have been the foundation of British liberties, and that any encroachment by the executive branch of government upon the independence of either was bound to raise the spectre of absolutism. On the other hand, the idea canvassed in other quarters of grafting on the British constitution a Bill of Rights taken from other constitutional and legal contexts showed an equal indifference to what had been one of the major sources of Britain's strength, the resilience and flexibility of its constitutional arrangements.

23.  Alan Macfarlane, *The Origins of English Individualism* (Oxford: 1978).
24.  J. C. D. Clark, *English Society, 1688–1832* (Cambridge: 1985).
25.  Max Beloff, *Wars and Welfare: Britain, 1914–1945* (London: 1984).

Nevertheless, neither the protection of individual rights nor Parliamentary government in any of its modes is of the essence of the British experience. It was indeed curious to see the formation of a 'multi-party system' being regarded as the touchstone of an acceptable substitute for the overthrow of communist regimes in eastern Europe or indeed elsewhere in the world. Competing political parties and the possibility they give of replacing an out-worn government through the ballot-box rather than by force are of course useful guarantees for internal peace.[26] But they have historically been late-comers even in the west, not excluding Britain. Much more important has been the development of regular forms of executive government. The tendency of intellectuals of a left-wing persuasion to mock 'law and order' as a slogan fit only for purblind reactionaries demonstrates an ignorance of history which is hard to take, particularly from those who at the same time insist on the importance of economic growth so as to provide the wherewithal to tackle the social problems to which they call attention.

If one looks at the history of England from the time of the Saxon kings, it is the ways in which an order enforced by the monarchy, and in which the Normans and Plantagenets built upon the earlier foundations of the 'king's peace', that must be the central theme. Economic development is dependent on civil peace. Unless people can peaceably go about their business, there will be no business for them to go about. And that can be achieved only if there is a monopoly of force in the hands of the ruler, an objective not fully attained in England until Tudor times but never lost to sight.

The second theme must be the establishment of known laws and of courts through which they can be enforced. The separation of the judicial from the executive role of the monarch, which came early in medieval England, has been equally essential to the country's ability to prosper. Only when the boundaries of the permitted are clear and no arbitrary act of the executive can alter them can people safely invest in agriculture, industry or commerce. As long as there exists the possibility of an arbitrary

---

26.  My belief that the chief use of political parties is to enable one government to be replaced by another explains my undeviating hostility to proportional representation, which tends to prevent the electorate from making such choices. I shall deal with this question more specifically when I come to discuss the case of Israel in a later chapter.

invasion of their rights and an absence of any court to which they can safely appeal for redress, no one is going to undertake the risks inherent in all enterprise. The problems of transition in eastern Europe (and in the former Soviet Union) from a command economy which has demonstrably failed to a market economy are not primarily economic but legal. Until one has a legal system enabling property to be defined and protected and contracts to be made and honoured, whether between persons or between persons and the state, economic progress whether based on internal or external investment is not possible.

Historically the incursions of the executive (that is, in medieval or early-modern England, the monarchy) have been connected with taxation. In order to give society room to breathe it was essential that there should be agreed limits to the right to tax. Limitations were at first imposed by the countervailing power of the feudatories and later by Parliament, in which the landowners' power was incorporated together with that of the other financially significant social strata.

By the eighteenth century, the importance of the regularity of taxation as the foundation of a prosperous economy was fully appreciated by Britain's ruling classes and formed the basis of their handling of their newfound empire in the east.[27] But the separation of powers between the executive and the legislature was to prove only temporary, though prominent enough to inspire foreign commentators and the makers of the American Constitution.

The last two centuries have seen the subordination of Parliament to the executive, to which power has largely been assigned, as is common among countries enjoying universal suffrage. And this in turn gives greater salience to the judiciary, since it is only the judiciary that can now control the use by the executive of the delegated powers it is able to extract from Parliament. Judicial review is thus the most important constitutional innovation of recent decades, which may explain the desire of the executive to bring the judiciary also under its control.

A view of British history that concentrates on the executive branch, on Whitehall rather than Westminster, is one that has grown upon me over the years and figures in much of my writing.

27.  C. A. Bayly, *Indian Society and the Making of the British Empire, The New Cambridge History of India*, 2/1 (Cambridge: 1988).

For earlier years, it may be the product of long immersion in the voluminous studies of British administration in the Middle Ages by T. F. Tout of the Manchester University history school.[28] It was certainly relevant to my work on the problems of public order in the later Stuart period, to which I have already referred. It coloured my approach to the study of British history in the inter-war period.[29] And it contributed to my early appreciation of the impact upon British administration that would be made by the increasingly multi-faceted relationship between the British government and international institutions, even before Britain became a signatory of the Treaty of Rome.[30] It was to be the focus of my attention as a teacher during my tenure of the Gladstone Chair of Government and Public Administration at Oxford.[31]

To take a 'Whitehall' (or for that matter a 'Westminster') approach to the history of this country has become very un-fashionable in recent years – unfashionable on the right because it seems to leave out the contribution to wealth-creation of the entrepreneurs and on the left because it seems to omit the pains and joys of the common people. I would not contest the view that the well-being of the ordinary citizen should be the prime objective of government and that is from the individual and voluntary activity that progress has come. Good government cannot of itself create well-being; but we have only to look around today's world to see that bad government can most surely destroy it.

One difficulty in the way of a full appreciation of the role of civil servants has been the lack of information about them as individuals compared with the enormous amount that can be gathered about their political masters. Britain is unusually rich in political biography. Biographies of civil servants are necessarily rare and not often illuminating. Only one masterpiece falls into

28.  T. F. Tout, *Chapters in Administrative History in Medieval England*, 6 vols (Manchester: 1920–31). His spirit was still palpable at Manchester when I went there to teach ten years after his death, and his close colleague James Tait was still about.
29.  Max Beloff, 'The Whitehall Factor: The Role of the Higher Civil Service', in Gillian Peele and Chris Cook (eds) *The Politics of Reappraisal, 1918–1939* (London: Macmillan, 1975).
30.  Max Beloff, *New Dimensions in Foreign Policy* (London: 1961).
31.  See my Oxford inaugural lecture in 1958, *The Tasks of Government* (Oxford: 1958); republished in Preston King (ed.), *The Study of Politics* (London: 1977).

that category, Arthur Bryant's *Samuel Pepys*, which enlivened my undergraduate reading.[32] And that owes much to the fact that Pepys was so committed and frank a diarist.[33] With the development of stricter codes of conduct after the mid-Victorian reforms, diaries by civil servants became frowned upon. Indeed that exemplar of the modern civil servant, Edward Bridges (Lord Bridges), wished them to be prohibited and set an example in this respect by confiding little of his vast experience to paper.[34] Most light on how things are actually done has been thrown by the writings of those whose Whitehall career has been only an intermittent interruption to other pursuits.[35]

It is important to appreciate how different is the functioning of government from its textbook models and how hard it is to describe it as it proceeds. So long as one sticks to the law of the constitution one can say at any one time what it is, with due caution as to doubtful cases upon which the courts have not given their view. And even the law textbooks need continuous updating. To go further and say this is how policies are formed, this is the input that goes into them, this is the balance between ministers and civil servants, this is where Parliament makes its contribution – to say any of this with confidence is to take major risks both that one is wrong at the time of writing and that, even if one is right, things will have moved on when the work reaches publication. All this I learned when collaborating in the writing of a textbook on British government.[36] And it is a truth not confined of course to British government alone.[37]

Such arguments do not imply that all attempts at descriptive writing about a country and its politics are without value. On the

32.  Arthur Bryant, *Samuel Pepys*, 3 vols (Cambridge: 1933–5), (reissued London: 1984–5).
33.  R. C. Latham and W. Matthews (eds), *The Diary of Samuel Pepys*, 11 vols (London: 1970–83).
34.  See the study of Bridges in Richard Chapman, *Ethics in the British Civil Service* (London: 1988).
35.  See e.g. Edwin Plowden (Lord Plowden), *An Industrialist in the Treasury: The Post-War Years* (London: 1989).
36.  Max Beloff and Gillian R. Peele, *The Government of the United Kingdom* (London: 1980; 2nd edn, *The Government of the U.K.*, 1985).
37.  My belief that this was so was strengthened by my experience of being joint general editor of the series in which *The Government of the United Kingdom* appeared, which meant responsibility for books on France, Italy, Canada, Japan, Germany, India and post-British Africa. What can be thought of studies of Soviet government written before 1985 or even 1991?

contrary, if to close acquaintance with the subject matter is allied a lapidary style, the impact may be considerable. Such was the case of Walter Bagehot's *The English Constitution*, published in 1867, which not merely made an impact upon his own con- temporaries but has continued to colour subsequent approaches to the subject until our own time, it having in the interval been many times reprinted.[38] Since it was published in German within a year of its British publication and in Spanish in 1902, it must also have had its impact abroad. Yet Bagehot himself in his introduction to the second British edition, published in 1872, described the difficulties in what he had tried to do:

> A contemporary writer who tries to paint what is before him is puzzled and perplexed; what he sees is changing daily. He must paint it as it stood at some one time, or else he will be putting side by side in his representations things which never were contemporaneous in reality. The difficulty is greater because a writer who deals with a living government naturally compares with the most important living governments and these are changing too; what he illustrates are altered in one way, and his sources of illumination probably in a different way.

The intention of the book as it stood at the time of the first edition was, he wrote, to:

> describe the English Constitution as it stood in the years 1865 and 1866. Roughly speaking it describes its working as it was in the time of Lord Palmerston; and since that time there have been many changes, some of spirit and some of detail. In so short a period there have rarely been more changes.[39]

Bagehot was certain that the effect of the Second Reform Act of 1867, would be very great but it was too soon to know what it would be. Looking back it is clear that the principal effect was to change the situation of members of Parliament in subordinating them to party discipline to a hitherto unknown degree, so that (particularly after the further increase in the franchise less than twenty years later) the whole prominence given by Bagehot to

38. The best edition is that in volume 5 of *The Collected Works of Walter Bagehot*, ed. Norman St John Stevas (Lord St John of Fawsley) (London: 1974).
39. *Ibid.*, p. 165.

the role of the House of Commons in choosing and sustaining ministries became obsolete.[40]

Bagehot's understanding of the institutions of his own time has of course been an inspiration to later writers. In particular the Labour cabinet minister Richard Crossman always cherished, as he told me and others, the ambition of becoming a latterday Bagehot and tried out his skill in various lectures and seminars. But pressures of politics and his premature death meant that the only note of substance that remains is his introduction to a reprint of Bagehot's own book.[41]

Such an admission of the value of an attempt at a description applies only to men who, like Bagehot or to an even greater extent Crossman, were fully acquainted with the political scene from the inside. I found after some time in the House of Lords that most of what I had written about that part of our system and indeed much else in the first edition of my textbook required alteration in the light of what I now knew. I have even less confidence in the possibility of a useful contribution to our understanding by what is termed 'political science', a brand of inquiry owing much to the sense of inferiority felt by all 'social scientists' towards those engaged in the natural sciences, where measurement is the essence, and much also to a wish to emulate and be acceptable to 'political scientists' in the United States.

Much effort and research money have gone into attempts to quantify aspects of Britain's political behaviour, and no doubt some of the discoveries about voters and their responses could be useful to those politicians whose principal concern is to secure the success of their own party. But there is no evidence that such sophistication has made politicians any more competent at solving the country's problems or even at forecasting the impact upon opinion of their actions or words. The overlap between academic 'political science', the pollsters, the media and the advertising agencies is not necessarily a healthy one, though it may help

40.  It must be assumed that the ambition of those who would break down the two-party system through the device of proportional representation is to restore the House of Commons to its role in Palmerston's time. It is difficult to see how this could be reconciled with the modern demand for programmes of legislation.
41.  Walter Bagehot, *The English Constitution*, ed. R. H. S. Crossman (London: 1963). According to his biographer, Crossman wished to sound a warning against the atrophy of Cabinet government. Anthony Howard, *Crossman: The Pursuit of Power* (London: 1990), p. 265.

academics to eke out the straitened incomes upon which an uncaring state expects them to live.

Such a digression brings us back to the main contention of this chapter. Britain, like other societies, can be understood only in terms of its own historical experience and of the interpretation of that experience by the people and their rulers. And it is of the essence of history that it is time-based. At its simplest, history is an account of events which have taken place one after another over a given period of time – in Britain for practical purposes over a couple of millennia. No event can be understood except in relation to what has gone before, and no action can be understood except in the light of two facts – that the actors knew or thought they knew what had gone before, and that they did not know and could not know what would be the consequences of what they did. It may be that there never was a Metro-Goldwyn-Mayer epic in which the medieval commander declared to his troops, 'We are now going off to fight the hundred years' war;' but the moral still stands. Charles I did not begin the Civil War in the expectation of losing his head on the scaffold and Oliver Cromwell did not enter it in the expectation of becoming Lord Protector.

While this is of course only an application to British history of a general truth, it is particularly pertinent to the proper subject of this chapter, the distinctiveness of British history; for the temptation when confronted with so long and continuous a story to imagine that outcomes were intended is bound to be present. It may have been easier to succumb to this temptation in Macaulay's time when British pre-eminence in the world was so much more widely recognized, than it is now, at a time of genuine doubt about the stability of our society and its institutions, when we know that Britain's power and influence in the world have massively and precipitously declined; but the temptation remains.

Nevertheless the continuity of British and more specifically of English institutions is a genuine mark of distinctiveness and one which no serious study of the country's history can afford to neglect. Many things made this possible. Alone in Europe, Britain has never been subdued by foreigners since the Norman Conquest of the eleventh century.[42] All subsequent battles on British soil

---

42. W. C. Sellar and R. J. Yeatman were quite correct in their choice of '1066 and all that' as the title of their spoof history. But the jokes, all easily understood by schoolchildren of the inter-war years when British history was still taught along conventional lines, would not, I fear, raise a laugh today. Parody cannot be understood without a knowledge of the original.

have been fought between Englishmen or with the Scots and the Welsh. The consciousness of this fact, emphasized by the defeat of the Spanish Armada, is manifest in our literature as well as in the attitudes of our political leaders. John of Gaunt's evocation of England – 'this fortress built by Nature for herself' – was written eight years after the Armada.[43] Sometimes the importance of this immunity from invasion can be underestimated. It is often pointed out that the characters in Jane Austen's novels seem oblivious to the Napoleonic wars – but these wars, like Britain's other wars, were fought abroad. Mr Bennet and Mr Woodhouse were in no danger of having foreign soldiers billeted upon them.

It was this sense of security that, despite occasional outbreaks of xenophobia, enabled the English to assimilate successive waves of foreign migration with such relative ease so that they in their turn became moulded by the country's institutions. In the last half-century much has changed. Britain's invulnerability now depends upon the goodwill and co-operation of another and greater power. In parts of England foreign servicemen have been present in not inconsiderable numbers. The 'silver sea' is no longer an adequate moat. And in that respect the lessons of history may cease to apply. But without an understanding of the long periods in which the sea has so functioned, and of the self-generated social and institutional development which it made possible in those centuries, there is no making sense of our current predicaments. The need to effect changes renders the study of history no less essential.

43.  It is good to record that, unlike 1688, the defeat of the Armada was duly celebrated.

# III

## The Idea of France

*Toute ma vie je me suis fait une certaine idée de la France.*
Charles de Gaulle

*The further off from England the nearer is to France.*
Lewis Carroll

Lewis Carroll was right. For the Englishman throughout the
centuries, it is France that has provided the main antithesis to his
fundamental beliefs. To be foreign is first and foremost to be
French. The dynastic interlocking of the two countries and the
wars to which this gave rise – the stuff of Shakespeare's historical
plays – ended when Mary Tudor finally abandoned England's last
possession on the mainland. But even when dynastically separate,
what went on in France could not be ignored. While England
developed its constitutional system, France reached the apogee
of royal absolutism, and the English king himself became a
pensionary of Louis XIV. When France was plunged into revolution and carried that revolution to most of the rest of continental
Europe, Britain stamped out the embers of revolution at home
and was the core of the continued resistance to the Napoleonic
hegemony. The preoccupation with France and the Anglo-French
rivalry continued until the making of the entente at the beginning
of the present century and has not been absent since.

For the historian this preoccupation with France and the
French is a welcome invitation. I have always held that French
history is the most interesting history we have at our disposal
and at one time cherished the idea of writing a history of the
Third Republic.[1] Again, my acquisition of this taste was largely

---

1. It is probably a good thing I did not proceed with this idea. I never acquired
   the intimacy with the country which enabled my teacher Denis Brogan to
   write his major work which appeared in the year that the Third Republic
   collapsed in the disaster of defeat; D. W. Brogan, *The Development of
   Modern France, 1870–1939* (London: 1940). I would also have been

accidental. It arose from my discovery as a schoolboy of the delights of French impressionist painting.[2] But the full realization of the degree to which impressionism itself was a key to French society in the years of its efflorescence had to await my quite recent reading of Robert L. Herbert's highly original study of the subject.[3]

Of course it would be an error to place too much emphasis on the origins of my impetus to concentrate on the Third Republic. Earlier schoolboy reading might have had a different effect. And it was not only Shakespeare. Scott's *Quentin Durward*, with its portrait of Louis XI, might have suggested the fifteenth century as a fertile ground for the imagination. When I got to the Loire Valley, the castle at Loches was my first target, and the fact that the prisoners' cages did not resemble the birdcage-style affairs illustrated in my Scott, the first disappointment. Chinon, the scene of Joan of Arc's legendary recognition of the Dauphin, might have taken me back to the earlier wars.[4] The proximity of the great Renaissance châteaux with their Italian echoes – long before I ever saw Italy – could have inspired a continued interest in the first period of French history in which, as with the Tudors in England, we begin to feel we are at grips with real people, not the formal contrivances of medieval chronicles. It was only when I first went to Edinburgh that I understood how desolate Mary Queen of Scots must have felt at exchanging the spaciousness of Renaissance France for the gloomy and confining rooms of Holyrood Palace.[5]

incapable of the extraordinary degree of learning and empathy which mark Theodore Zeldin's two volumes in *The Oxford History of Modern Europe*: Theodore Zeldin, *France, 1848–1945* (2 vols Oxford: 1973, 1977).

2.  I was thrilled when arriving at Manchester University as an assistant lecturer in 1939 to find this made me a colleague of R. H. Wilenski, whose writings had done so much to stir my interest in the subject.

3.  Robert L. Herbert, *Impressionism: Art, Leisure and Parisian Society* (New Haven and London: 1988).

4.  I am not in a position to think of Joan of Arc as an historical figure because my impression of her role and personality was coloured by having seen the first production of Bernard Shaw's *St Joan* in 1924, at the age of eleven. Henceforward, as far as I was concerned, Joan of Arc was Sybil Thorndike. This image was not even supplanted by that of Suzanne Flon in Jean Anouilh's very different play on the same theme, *L'Alouette*.

5.  What can be done to glamorize Mary Queen of Scots has been done by Donizetti in his *Maria Stuarda*, based on Schiller's version of her end. It is curious to what an extent Tudor and Stuart history, somewhat improved upon, has inspired Italian composers. There is nothing like it for French history.

And then of course there is the seventeenth century, when modern France begins to take shape in its geographical dimensions. Did I read *The Three Musketeers* before or after *Quentin Durrward*? I only know that as for Denis Brogan, who has chronicled the experience of reading *Twenty Years After*, this experience was an exciting one, leading me to read in the red-covered pocket volumes of the then available English translations many of its sequels.[6] Without even the background in conventional French history that a French boy of my age might be supposed to have, my picture of the years of the Fronde and of the early part of Louis XIV's reign must have been somewhat remote from the unvarnished truth. But better romantic history than no history at all.[7] In any event Lewis Carroll was absolutely justified.

De Gaulle was right also. Not only did he have a particular idea of France but so does everyone else who feels drawn to that country and its history. As I have indicated, my own interest was from the beginning with the Third Republic. Partly this was due to my own preference for the period in which political and social development was not interrupted by revolutionary violence. I have of course like other historians had to face the fact of the French Revolution and its impact on Europe.[8] But I never felt anything but a strong distaste for the revolutionaries, their ideas and their actions. How right I was I was not fully aware until among the flood of literature provoked by the 1789 anniversary celebrations I read the powerful work of Simon Schama.[9]

6. D. W. Brogan, 'Alexander the Great', in *French Personalities and Problems* (London: 1946).
7. As far as I can make out, neither Scott nor Dumas are read by English schoolchildren today. Instead they are fed, when they read at all, on a diet of books especially written for the juvenile market, of no literary value and offering no entry into the world of history. Their loss, but perhaps history's too. Even Baroness Orczy's *Scarlet Pimpernel* (1905), which perhaps dictated from my childhood a strong antipathy to the revolutionaries, while not great literature, is better than what the young read now.
8. How far the ideas of the French Revolution affected the rapid processes of change in the non-European world, I would be incompetent to judge. But interest in this aspect of the story may well be stimulated by C. A. Bayly, *Imperial Meridian: The British Empire and the World, 1780–1830* (London: 1989).
9. Simon Schama, *Citizens: A Chronicle of the French Revolution* (London: 1989). It is interesting to note that the French did not take to Schama. It was not translated. François Furet, *La Révolution, 1770–1880* (Paris: 1989), gives a longer perspective.

It was also attractive in that it was a field in which one's penchant for fiction could be indulged while feeling that one was enlarging one's social and political horizons. No book has made a greater impression on me than Jules Romains' now largely forgotten Les Hommes de bonne volonté, the twenty-seven volumes of which I successively acquired and read as they appeared over the years 1932–47 – those in wartime published in New York. Other romans fleuve also played a part in my understanding of the Third Republic – George Duhamel's Chronique des Pasquier (ten volumes acquired between 1933 and 1945) and Roger Martin Gard's Les Thibault (1922–40). Proust was a later taste, but George Painter's biography was a lead into the society of the earlier decades of the Republic which again helped to determine my interest and approach.[10]

Naturally such reading, even when fortified by a study of the French and British historians of the period, is no substitute for direct research. Where France is concerned, I have done painfully little of that. Indeed I have made only two contributions of any significance to the subject. One was a study of the riots of 1934 that looked as though they might end the Republic and substitute a more authoritarian regime of the type increasingly fashionable in Europe of the 1930s.[11] The other was a study partly from private sources of the abortive Anglo-French Union project of 1940.[12]

It is of course the case that modern France does not begin with 1870 and although I have not overcome my aversion to the Revolution, the period of the Restoration and the July Monarchy does invite attention and provide the background to the makers of the Third Republic itself.

It is a natural tendency for the British to see that period through the eyes of the French liberals, above all of Tocqueville. Indeed the reciprocity of feeling and understanding between French and British liberals is one aspect of the complicated intellectual relationship between the two countries throughout much of the nineteenth century.[13] Tocqueville himself has been the

10.  George D. Painter, Proust, 2 vols (London: 1959, 1965; 2nd edn, 1989).
11.  'The Sixth of February', reprinted from St Antony's Papers, vol. V (1959) in Max Beloff, The Intellectual in Politics and Other Essays (London: 1970).
12.  'The Anglo-French Union Project of 1940', reprinted from Mélanges: Pierre Renouvin (Paris: 1966) in Beloff, The Intellectual in Politics.
13.  See Max Beloff, 'The Impact of the French Revolution upon British Statecraft, 1789–1921', in Ceri Crossley and Ian Small (eds), The French Revolution and British Culture (Oxford: 1989).

subject of much study and comment in France over recent years.[14] And this attention is fully justified by the scope of his interests and the penetration of his thought. Nevertheless there is a warning to be given.

Tocqueville's main historical insights were derived from his study of the *ancien régime*, intended to be a prelude to the study of the Revolution itself. His purpose was to show that the Revolution and Napoleon only deepened and made more effective the existing French tendency to ever greater centralization. It is therefore tempting to follow French liberals in contrasting such centralization with the emphasis on locality and local self-government which they regarded as characteristic of the 'Anglo-Saxons'.[15] And no doubt there existed in nineteenth-century France an apparatus of government which at least on paper was rivalled only by Prussia.[16] But more detailed research on a local basis suggests that the actual reach of government was far less effective in many parts of the country, especially in rural areas, than this view would suggest.[17] If Tocqueville had been as familiar with Brittany or the Massif Central or the south-west as he was with Normandy and the Ile de France, might not his outlook have had to be modified?

Considerations of the degree to which France was effectively centralized from an administrative point of view are closely connected with another and more delicate topic, that of the persistence over the centuries of a single identifiable French nation seeking its 'natural' boundaries and expressing through successive dynasties and regimes its distinctive national spirit. Such was the content of the formal French historiography as relayed to the schools during the formative years of the Third Republic. The new currents in historical writing which made themselves felt even before 1914 and which reached their fruition in the inter-

---

14. Since the new edition of *Oeuvres complètes* began publication in 1959, twenty-four volumes have appeared and it is still not complete. Recent scholarship is well summed up by one of the editors, André Jardin, in his *Alexis de Tocqueville* (Paris: 1984).
15. Max Beloff, 'Tocqueville et l'Angleterre', in *Alexis de Tocqueville: Livre du Centenaire* (Paris: 1960).
16. For the eighteenth-century origins of the French and Prussian systems, see C. B. A. Behrens, *Society, Government and the Enlightenment: The Experience of Eighteenth-Century France and Prussia* (London: 1985).
17. For this insight and much of what follows, I am indebted to the truly remarkable work by Eugen Weber, *Peasants into Frenchmen: The Modernization of Rural France* (London: 1977).

war period were bound to criticize such a teleological view, and to emphasize that modern France as consolidated in the Third Republic was the product of particular historical changes and that alternative associations and an alternative political geography had been available at many earlier junctures.[18] In this light, the accepted heroic figures of the nation's history as written in the romantic period – Joan of Arc for instance – appear in a new light.

Eugen Weber has gone further in pointing to the fact that the famous hexagon itself consisted of territories added to the Capetian core partly by dynastic alliances but mainly by conquest over the centuries:

> in the thirteenth century, Languedoc and parts of the center; in the fifteenth Acquitaine and Provence; in the sixteenth Brittany; in the seventeenth Navarre, Béarn, Pays Basque, Roussillon and Cerdagne, parts of Alsace and French Flanders, Franche Comté; in the eighteenth the Duchy of Lorraine, Corsica, the Papal Comté Venaissin; in the nineteenth Savoy and Nice.[19]

And these provinces were seats of separate languages or at least patois with different cultural traditions, different external points of reference and often indigenous local institutions. To many of Michelet's 'French' contemporaries, French was a foreign language, though one with no serious literary rival. Only at the end of the nineteenth century with the completion of the railway system, with the impact of universal and largely lay schooling and of universal military conscription did the school and barracks produce the relatively homogeneous France that went to war in 1914 and recovered the lost provinces of 1871. And even then the process of unification was incomplete, and in some cases may be incomplete today.

The scepticism of some of the new school of historians regarding the very existence of France as a subject for historical inquiry was not universal among them. Marc Bloch, himself the descend-

---

18.   See the review article of 1933 by Lucien Febvre, 'Ni histoire à thèse – ni histoire manuel: entre Benda et Seignobos', which deals with Julien Benda, *Esquisse d'une histoire des français dans leur volonté d'être une nation* (Paris: 1932) and C. Seignobos, *Histoire sincère de la nation française: essai d'une histoire de l'évolution du peuple français* (Paris: 1933).
19.   Weber, *Peasants into Frenchmen*, p. 485.

ant of Jews of the long-established community in Alsace, who was critical of all parochialism during his tenure of a post at the University of Strasbourg after its recovery from the Germans, was not merely a French patriot in the tradition of his family but also very directly concerned with the particular contribution of France to the society of the west. The fall of France in 1940, after he had been called to arms for the second time in his life, led him to a study of the causes of France's defeat and to participation in the Resistance, resulting in his death at the hands of the occupier. He certainly did not doubt that there was something essentially French in the ideas to which he was devoted. In his *L'Etrange Défaite* written after the débâcle of 1940, he appeared as 'the aggrieved patriot who spared himself and his beloved France no pain'.[20]

Fernand Braudel, who inherited the mantle of Febvre and Bloch, made his name as we have seen with a study of the Mediterranean world and was equally at home in the archives and among the peoples of all that world. Yet he too was to end his career with an unfinished masterpiece seeking to explain what had made France the country that it is over the long centuries of settlement and development since earliest times.[21]

What the French have found looking at their history can be roughly channelled into two themes. One has been the persistent impact of France upon the rest of the world and in particular Europe. To call a history of the Crusades, *Gesta Dei per Francos* was to set an example that would be followed long after the crusading impulse had faded and when the country's objectives were more secular. The search for glory in foreign conquests that followed the consolidation of the French state by Louis XI was in many respects very demanding and costly. But the military prestige of France and its diplomatic triumphs went alongside the progressive diffusion of its language and ideas. French became and remained until very recently the ordinary language of international intercourse, as Latin had been before it. It also became in the eighteenth century the lingua franca of the aristocracy and the cultivated classes generally as far afield as Russia. No doubt other countries had their share in the intellectual achievements of the

20.   See Carole Fink, *Marc Bloch: A life in History* (Cambridge: 1989), p. 237.
21.   Fernand Braudel, *L'Identité de la France*, 3 vols (Paris: 1986), which has not had an English translation.

Enlightenment, but its core was unmistakably French. When the French armies and Napoleon's viceroys spread the new ideas of the Revolution thoughout most of Europe, leaving an indelible imprint on its laws and institutions, they were cultivating ground already tilled by their predecessors under the *ancien régime*.[22]

The other principal theme of modern French history is the opposite one. While to the outside world France represented for much of the modern period a vital distillation of military and political power and a source of intellectual inspiration, it was itself deeply divided not merely by objective factors analysed by Eugen Weber, town versus country, Paris and standard French versus provinces and patois, nor even by the divisions between classes both as congealed in the *ancien régime* and as remodelled by industrialization, but also and most obviously in the realm of ideas. Frenchmen are perhaps among European peoples those who have been the most divided by ideology and the most prone to persecute in its name.

The first internal divisions of this kind since the thirteenth-century destruction of the Albigensians were those created by the Protestant Reformation. The Wars of Religion in France were marked by brutality as great as that to be found anywhere in the Europe of the time. The Massacre of St Bartholomew became a by-word for ideological savagery until outclassed in our own day.[23] During the seventeenth century, with the Catholic victory assured, the armed struggle was intermittent. In Louis XIV's reign, the revocation of the Edict of Nantes putting an end to guarantees given to the Protestant minority earlier in the century produced a new wave of persecution and an emigration of the affected minority which were to have far-reaching consequences for French society. They may help to explain the extreme anticlericalism and eventual repudiation of Christianity itself which were to foreign critics of the Revolution like Edmund Burke its most damaging and incomprehensible aspect.

22.  For an account of the French impact on one of France's conquests, see Simon Schama, *Patriots and Liberators: Revolution in the Netherlands, 1780–1813* (London: 1972)
23.  The diffusion of the accounts of the Massacre of St Bartholomew throughout Europe marked the first use of the printing press to diffuse a martyrology and to justify a theory of resistance to tyranny. In 1972, French Protestants commemorated its 400th anniversary and, in 1985, the 300th anniversary of the revocation of the Edict of Nantes. See R. M. Kingdom, *Myths about the St Bartholomew's Massacre, 1572–1576* (Cambridge, Mass.: 1988).

Clearly it was the Revolution that did most to intensify existing divisions and to create new ones. In the course of a few short years it not only crystallized the divisions between monarchism and republicanism, between the rights of property and socialism, between bourgeois and proletarians, between Catholic and the lay interpretations of past and present, but gave France and the rest of Europe the vocabulary of modern politics, which in the case of classical concepts like aristocracy and democracy distorted them for good. Names of the months designed to break with the theocratic past acquired political significance – Thermidor, Brumaire. All subsequent revolutions were thought of in terms of its sequence of stages. Even after the failure of the Second Empire, 'Bonapartism' remained embedded in the European revolutionary consciousness. The process of encapsulating in words different tendencies within the body politic had been completed during the Restoration when 'liberal' and 'conservative' became current not merely in France but throughout continental Europe. Even Britain could not hold out for ever, and by mid-century Liberal and Conservative replaced the historical Whig and Tory.

It was this deep embodiment in France of the basic ideas of the Revolution and the Counter-Revolution that made the controversies over the historical interpretation of the events themselves so crucial to later political debate.[24] But it was not only at the level of scholarship that this was true. The domination of primary education by the Church was something the victorious Republicans of 1870 were determined to end. After all for so many Frenchmen the texts set at school were the only books they would ever read. In the period between the establishment of a national system of education and the war of 1914–18, school books were designed to inculcate a lay version of patriotism; religious figures in France's past and her great cathedrals went unmentioned. Only Joan of Arc survived the purge. In this as in so much else, the war marked the beginning of a new era. The revulsion its losses inspired resulted in the emergence of a new generation of teachers, pacifist and socialist in their allegiance. The old republican patriotism went the way of France the champion of Christendom. The working class and its exploitation

24. See for a modern summary of the debate, François Furet, *Penser la Révolution française* (Paris: 1978), and *La Révolution de Turgot à Jules Ferry, 1770–1880* (Paris: 1988).

became the central theme of social study, and, since military leaders were taboo, French children had to adopt as role-models explorers and sportsmen.[25]

One result of the concentration on the cementing force of ideologies in the earlier years of the Third Republic was the coming together of the left in the shape of the Radical Party founded in 1901 and the Unified Socialist Party of 1905. For these parties and their co-operation a vital catalyst had been the Dreyfus case and its sequels.[26]

These political developments contained much myth-making, particularly on the left:

> Mythological history recorded no socialist indifference, no radical hesitations, but a spontaneous mobilization for the Republic, innocence and justice against militarism, chauvinism and anti-Semitism – hitherto no stranger to the Left but henceforth at least officially anathema. Against clericalism too which was taken to represent not just hostility to progress but also the equivalent of a political party, the only organized political force in the land.[27]

Neither side in the struggle was as united as its opponents would have us believe. General de Gaulle's father, a devoted Catholic of monarchist sympathies, refused to go along with the anti-Dreyfus clamour or to accept the nascent violence of part of the right. De Gaulle's own political affinities in the inter-war years are also distinctly complicated and do not easily fit into the conventional models of a right-wing officer caste.[28] For the pre-1914 period, fiction is a useful guide. Roger Martin du Gard's novel *Jean Barois*, written on the eve of the war but only published

25.   J. Emelina, 'La Littérature de l'Ecole primaire: l'idéologie des livres courante dans l'enseignement primaire en France depuis la III[e] Republique', in M. Yardeni (ed.), *Idéologie et propagande en France* (Paris: 1983).
26.   For a modern account of the Dreyfus affair and its impact see Jean-Louis Bredin, *L'Affaire* (Paris: 1983). The initial hesitations of most of the socialist groupings and their leaders at taking part in what they saw as a struggle between two sections of the bourgeoisie and the steps by which most of them under the leadership of Jaurès became identified with the Dreyfusards is dealt with in the chapter 'French Socialism and the Dreyfus Affair' in Robert Wistrich, *Between Redemption and Perdition: Modern Anti-Semitism and the Jewish Identity* (London: 1990).
27.   Eugen Weber, *France: Fin de siècle* (Cambridge, Mass.: 1986), p. 239.
28.   For an introduction to this aspect of the politics of the period it would be hard to better the first volume of Jean Lecouture, *De Gaulle*, 3 vols (Paris: 1984–6).

in 1917, treats of the transformation of the original campaign for justice for Dreyfus into an instrument for the exploitation of political anti-clericalism to bring about the unity of the left. It also traces the emergence among a younger generation of a new right-wing politics bringing Catholicism and republican patriotism back together.

*Jean Barois* also points to another specifically French feature of the politics of the time. The progress of the natural sciences and the incorporation of their basic notions into the general outlook of educated society were relatively easy in Britain and other Protestant countries – despite Disraeli's famous dismissal of Darwinism. In France however the new discoveries and theories, because of the hostility to them of the Church, became involved in the general battle between ideologies and institutions. And this may help to explain the significance attached to 'intellectuals' in the public life of France, which Eugen Weber sees as having subsided after the 1850s but as reviving as a consequence of the Dreyfus case.[29]

Myth-making has been necessary in even more recent times. The degree to which many Frenchmen in all walks of life not merely accepted the Vichy regime but actively collaborated with the German occupying forces had somehow to be expunged from the national consciousness if the country's pride was to be restored. It was not an easy task and is still incomplete.

After the Liberation there was the extraordinary complicity of so many French intellectuals in the exaltation of the Soviet and other communist regimes, a new manifestation of their favourite slogan 'Pas d'ennemis à gauche'. How in the light of all the revelations about the hollowness of the Soviet system such spurious eminences as Jean-Paul Sartre contrived to keep their reputation and their following is something with which future historians will have to cope. Much credit is due to the one major figure who never compromised with this nonsense, Raymond Aron, whom it was my privilege to know, though not intimately. He redeemed the reputation of the French intelligentsia.[30]

29. Weber, *France*, p. 239.
30. R. Colquhoun, *Raymond Aron*, 2 vols (London: 1986), is an uninspired but very useful account of Aron's life and writings, though not to be compared with Aron's own *Mémoires* (Paris: 1983). Apart from Aron himself, I owe my interest in French politics to acquaintances among French political scientists: Bertrand de Jouvenel, Maurice Duverger, François Goguel and André Mathiot among others.

In the 1980s, with the successive revelations within the Soviet Union of the horrors and imbecilities of the system, Marxism began to lose its hold France. And this weakening of what had almost become an orthodoxy again brought the problem of interpreting the Revolution to the fore, quite apart from the imminence of the bicentenary.

It has also been argued that the shift from a sociological explanation of the event to one with an emphasis on the political choice was given an added impetus by the Paris upheaval of 1968, when the absurdly self-important international student movement of the 1960s with its epicentre in Berkeley, California suddenly irrupted into the real world:

> for a few days, revolution suddenly seemed possible – not revolution conceived as a rather mechanical change of political regime or as a necessary end result of a conflict between social classes, but revolution experienced as an ultimate moment of political choice, in which the givens of social existence seemed suspended, the only power was the power of the imagination and the world could be made anew.[31]

For this pantomime helped the author of these lines and other historians both in France and abroad to look again at the political conflicts of the last years of the monarchy. They noted the elaboration in those decades of the ideas and language that were to lead the revolutionaries after some hesitation to adopt the theory of the general will embodied in themselves and so make way for the Terror. Such an outcome of the first two years of constitution-making – 1789–90 – also implied the rejection of the two available and much discussed Anglo-Saxon models. The French did not choose to follow the English example of 1688–9 by accepting the continuity of the country's institutions, including the monarchy, while introducing new elements to strengthen an endangered balance, nor like the Americans did they limit themselves to the political and administrative sphere while leaving 'civil society' untouched.

Because the Revolution rejected history and claimed to be beginning everything anew, even the calendar, it could by its votaries be seen as of universal application. The armies of the

31.  Keith Michael Baker, *Inventing the French Revolution: Essays on French Political Culture in the Eighteenth Century* (Cambridge: 1990), p. 3.

Revolution and of Bonaparte were to carry these ideas to most of
the rest of Europe and to leave even in the countries which
rebelled against French pretensions and French exactions a sedi-
ment that two centuries have not wholly dissipated.

I have mentioned in passing my own exploration of the Anglo-
French Union project of 1940 which I embarked upon when asked
to contribute to a *Festschrift* in honour of Pierre Renouvin, with
whom I was collaborating in a collective history of nineteenth-
and twentieth-century Europe. It was in the immediate post-war
years that I was most often in France and got to know some of the
principal historians of that time. In fact, however, this interest
had arisen in part at least from contacts I had had with exiled
French in London who mainly, though not exclusively, under de
Gaulle's banner were striving to make sure, despite Vichy, that
France would contribute to an Allied victory and end the war as
one of the victors.

Of all the vicissitudes in Anglo-French relations over the
centuries the episode of de Gaulle's sojourn in London and the
story of his difficult relations with Churchill stand alone for their
importance and complexity. Wisely committed to seeing French
power and influence restored, rightly also suspicious of the Vichy
regime, Churchill was inhibited not only by de Gaulle's extreme
and understandable insistence upon a degree of acceptance that
neither his personal position nor the strength of the forces at his
disposal could justify, but in addition by the very hostile attitude
of Roosevelt, too long a victim of his advisers' tenderness for
Vichy, and later on too prone to think that French political life
could await Liberation and a period of direct Allied control before
its framework was fixed.

My contacts with the French on my visits to London between
1941 and 1943 when the theatre of events moved decisively to
Algiers were too intermittent and my knowledge of French politics
too limited to make me aware of the inwardness of what was going
on, as de Gaulle built up his control of the French in the empire
and abroad, and established himself as the leader of the internal
Resistance (whose ramifications were of course secret). The story

32.  I look back with little pride upon the most widely read of my own books,
     *The Age of Absolutism*, studied by generations of sixth-formers since it was
     published in 1954; but reading Professor Baker's book I did at least derive
     the satisfaction of seeing that the dates I used for this period of European
     history, 1660–1815, were probably right.

has recently been told again, though with less local detail than the title would lead one to expect, in a book by two French historians, *La France à Londres*.[33]

For some people in Britain the re-establishment of France was an important British war aim, and the struggle of de Gaulle a source of inspiration. One such individual was the journalist and historian J. L. Hammond, who had returned at the beginning of the war to full-time work on the *Manchester Guardian*, still a great Liberal newspaper. Hammond, who had made his name on the pro-Boer wing of the Liberal Party at the turn of the century, was by now in his seventies, but his earlier enthusiasms were stirred by the attention he devoted to the struggle over France.[34] His editorials on the subject from June to September 1940, like his conversation, were of an intensity so passionate that the various Liberal causes he had espoused came together.[35]

Such experiences are bound to be racalled in something of a spirit of irony; nothing came out as intended. It can hardly be denied that France's eventual appearance at the founding of the United Nations and as one of the powers that drew up the new map of Europe which was to last forty years owed much to Britain, and to Churchill in particular, and that much effort went into overcoming the familiar divergences that had marred the relations of the two countries in the recent past, for instance in the

33.   Michèle et Jean-Paul Cointet, *La France à Londres* (Paris: 1990). It is curious but not untypical that in a book set in London many English names are misspelled and English titles of organizations mistranslated. The concern of the French for the purity of their own language is not always paralleled by respect for other peoples' languages. Vol. 1 of Lacouture, *De Gaulle*, is again of the first importance.

34.   It remains a lesson in the relativity of ideologies that while admiration for the Boers was a mark of a true liberal in Hammond's younger days, he was to live to see the triumph of the Afrikaner, i.e. Boer nationalism in the South African election of 1948, after which no one could be regarded as a liberal in Britain unless he was an avowed enemy of the Afrikaners. Yet they were the same people with the same views and the same prejudices.

35.   Hammond's editorials were published as *Faith in France* with a preface by D. W. Brogan (Manchester: 1946). The impetus for the publication came from Eugene Vinaver, Professor of French at the University of Manchester and the foremost authority on Sir Thomas Mallory. His father M. M. Vinaver was a leading figure among the post-Revolution Russian émigrés in Paris. He too had been a Liberal in that false Russian dawn at the beginning of the century. The history of Europe transcends national boundaries in unexpected ways.

Middle East. But de Gaulle never lost his belief that Britain was always likely to prefer its ties to the United States to any role in Europe. Once France was free of the Nazi yoke and once American strength had rendered unlikely its replacement by Soviet domination, France resumed its search for a fully in-dependent foreign policy and found itself by degrees more and more inclining to the view that relations with the new German Federal Republic were the key to that independence. While this new orientation was begun by de Gaulle's successors in the Fourth Republic, the process was not reversed after his return to power in 1958. Indeed the Suez affair of 1956 might be seen as the last occasion on which a Franco-British partnership operated – and then, alas, unsuccessfully.

One can of course explore *ad infinitum* the varied aspects of modern France. What is hard to define and yet must be part of the attraction of the subject is what is essentially French about France. For most people would admit that, while national character may be something incapable of definition, it is possible to feel that something belongs to a certain country and could emerge only from a particular national tradition. Having begun with remarks about painting (the most obvious example where France is concerned), I am tempted to end with music. When impressionism and post-impressionism were making their con-quests, a musical style emerged that was recognizably French.

While Paris was obviously a musical capital of importance in the eighteenth century and during the Restoration, it would generally be held that the two great musical traditions of Europe have been the German and the Italian. It is curious to find that the German composer Carl Maria von Weber should have written that no nation has 'been so slow and uncertain as the German in determining its own specific art forms',[36] and that he should have compared Germany's painful apprenticeship to the freedom with which the French as well as the Italians had developed their own operatic style. Paris was indeed to remain important as a centre for the performance of opera as it had been in the time of Gluck, but it is hard to see there was anything particularly French in the contributions of French composers to the Romantic repertoire of the middle of the nineteenth century; only Berlioz ranks with the

36.  Quoted by Harold James in *A German Identity, 1770–1890* (London: 1989), p. 24.

great. It is once again in the Third Republic that we get an unmistakable French imprint with Saint-Saëns, César Franck, Fauré, Debussy and Franck's pupil, Ravel. The prominence given to the composer Vinteuil in Proust reflects the overlap between the literary and musical worlds of his time. The national imprint is as strong on the one as on the other.

# IV

## The United States:
## The Repudiation of History

It might seem natural to proceed from studying the impact of French history upon the rest of the world to considering the history of the United States of America. The period during which France exercised leadership in the battle of ideas in the west ended with the débâcle of 1940. French politics since the Liberation have been distinctly inward-looking, the product both of defeat and of the failed reaction of the Vichy regime. On the other hand, the United States, whose revolution preceded that of France (which it indirectly helped to precipitate), now clearly came into its own as the major source of inspiration. If by the beginning of the 1990s some of the hopes placed in the United States had begun to fade and its own institutions to show serious signs of strain, American history was something which, after long neglect, Europe found it necessary to assimilate into its mental background. The proliferation of American studies – not without generous help from the United States – has been a feature of higher education in almost all countries of western Europe and latterly in eastern Europe, including the former Soviet Union.

I cannot pretend that my own involvement with these studies was due to any early insight into this changing intellectual map. Like most things it came about by accident. I had taken little advantage of the fact that I had as tutor and then colleague in Oxford one of the few British scholars of the time with an intimate knowledge of the American scene, Denis Brogan. When I went to Manchester to take up my first full-time teaching job in the autumn of 1939, it was with British and to a lesser degree French and western European history that I expected to be concerned. The war made inroads into the staff of what had been one of the major departments of history in the country; and I too went off after a year into the army. In my case, however, ill-health meant that my absence was not of long duration and in twelve months I was back. By this time, with the United States at last an ally, the clamour to make up for the neglect of American history in British universities was irresistible, and, since my presence was a kind of unexpected bonus, it was probably inevitable that, in army language, I should have been told to volunteer. Nor was there much room for choice as to the period of American history in which I should specialize. Not only had I some knowledge of the British background to the 'colonial period' but such books and materials as were available in Manchester's libraries were suited only to teaching the colonial period and the American Revolution itself. So for once I began at the beginning. If one's interests are political and the study of government is central to them, an early acquaintance with the life and work of the Founding Fathers is a very good start. In France for a time after 1789 the demagogues triumphed over the men of reason; in the United States, the reverse was true.

The direction of my interests having thus been externally determined, this was to prove true also of my own early publications in the field. The first was an edition of the *Federalist* papers which still seem to me a perpetual source of political wisdom.[1] The second was a contribution to a series of volumes on the history of political ideas in their relation to political action, in which I tried to show how the pamphlets and speeches in the American colonies and Britain at the time of the Revolution raised fundamental questions of political allegiance and representative government that were still alive.[2] But by 1949, when the volume appeared, I had begun another interest which has proved equally enduring when I was asked to write for a series of short biographies a volume on Thomas Jefferson.[3] One may agree or disagree with

1.  Alexander Hamilton, James Madison and John Jay, *The Federalist*, ed. by Max Beloff (Oxford: 1948; 2nd edn, 1987)
2.  Max Beloff (ed.), *The Debate on the American Revolution* (London: 1949; 2nd edn, 1960; 3rd edn, Dobbs Ferry, NY: 1989). I also wrote 'American Independence in Its Constitutional Aspects' as Chapter XVI in vol. 8 of *The New Cambridge Modern History* (Cambridge: 1965).
3.  Max Beloff, *Thomas Jefferson and American Democracy* (London: 1948). Such was the eagerness of the US government in the immediate post-war period to make great Americans better known that subsidized translations of the book

Jefferson's political ideas but he remains someone of endless fascination – the finest flower of the Enlightenment, and that in colonial Virginia.

By this time, I had moved back to Oxford, where the university in its roundabout way had decided to provide for the new interest in American studies by creating what was rather fancifully called a readership in 'the comparative study of institutions'. I had also paid my first visit to the United States; the preface to the Jefferson book is dated from the University of Minnesota. The need to liquidate a brief commitment to Soviet studies – another accidental result of my wartime free-floating status – prevented any immediate plunging into more serious work on the United States. And it was not until another decade had passed that I published the first results of my readership, a short book for the Home University Library on American political institutions.[4] My first and subsequent visits to the United States made me believe that, unless one is willing at least to divide one's life between the two sides of the Atlantic, first-rate original research by non-Americans into American history is well-nigh impossible. The Europe-based scholar cannot really compete with those who have the libraries and archives at hand. I know there are distinguished exceptions, but they are very few.

So, where American history was concerned, my energies went into teaching. Oxford had also tended to concentrate on the revolutionary period, to conform with the tastes of its first professor, Samuel Eliot Morison. But it was now decided to plunge further into American history proper and to offer an optional special subject in Slavery and Secession. In many respects this subject seems to me an ideal one for undergraduate study, and not for the reason which led some undergraduates to choose this option, namely that it needed no foreign language to handle the prescribed texts. It was, I think, ideal because it presented within the manageable compass of a decade or so the unfolding drama of a country's unwilling descent into civil war and because it illuminated the way in which the frame of government can determine the actions of individual personages in a drama of this kind. It also offered what undoubtedly appeals to the young when they

---

appeared in Italian, Spanish, Japanese and Chinese (twice in Chinese – one in Taiwan and one in Hong Kong).

4.   *The American Federal Government* (Oxford: 1959; 2nd edn, 1969).

embark seriously upon history: a distinctive set of moral problems. Jefferson may appeal to the sophisticated but Abraham Lincoln is a man for the young. Finally, the Civil War was a subject whose divisive potentialities had not been exhausted in American historiography, so that it provided the perfect introduction to the inevitable lack of finality in all historical judgements. My confidence in the merits of Slavery and Secession was fortified by the fact that among the undergraduates who passed through the course were several later appointed to chairs of American history as these began to be filled or created at other British universities.

For me there was another personal advantage. The Harmsworth chair of American history was filled by a visiting scholar for a year at a time. Sometimes, these scholars were themselves specialists in the Civil War period, sometimes not. But all were willing to help take a class to supplement individual tutorials which I and one or two other dons were giving. So I came to know many American scholars at the top of their profession, which was an education in itself, however belated. The names of some of them form an honours roll: Allan Nevins, Henry Steele Commager, Merrill Jensen, C. Vann Woodward, Walter Rostow, Arthur Link, Walter Johnson. Others like Merle Curti and J. S. Randall I got to know in America. It was a generation confident of the relevance of historical studies and without the self-conscious pedantry of some of their successors.

My own subsequent writing was limited in both subject matter and period. The post-war world was being moulded by American policy, sometimes with creative imagination, sometimes within self-inflicted intellectual limitations. The irruption of the United States on to the world scene at the turn of the century and its subsequent conduct in international affairs is a subject of inexhaustible interest. It had for me a link with earlier interests in that Tocqueville's *Democracy in America* was an Oxford set-book on which I lectured in successive years, and it was Tocqueville who drew attention both to the difficulty for a democracy of dealing with foreign affairs – a problem from which the United States was largely insulated by the particular constellation of world affairs in Tocqueville's time – and also to the likely rivalry in the future of the United States and Russia as two competing world powers.

My first attempt to get to grips with the problems of American conduct of foreign policy was in a series of lectures written at the Institute for Advanced Study at Princeton and delivered at Johns

Hopkins University at Baltimore.[5] Later at the Brookings Institution in Washington I focused more specifically on the role of United States in the movement leading to the creation of the European Communities and tried to explore the ambiguities in American policy in this area – ambiguities which have taken a new twist with the ending of the direct east–west confrontation.[6]

A question of particular concern was that of Anglo-American relations. For professional reasons there was every temptation to accept the 'special relationship' as a fact, since it would help explain the ready acceptance of British academics by their American counterparts. Yet I felt it was too far to jump from this position to what some of my colleagues appeared to think, namely that Anglo-American harmony was something destined to grow despite the very obvious differences between the two societies and their ideologies and the occasional direct clash of interests.[7]

As later on I became more immersed in the imperial aspect of British history it was evident that it was here that one would find one of the great gulfs between the two countries.[8] It was of course the case that some Americans, at a time when their country was entering upon an expansive phase, looked with some admiration upon the British Empire. One such had been Theodore Roosevelt, who for a time replaced Thomas Jefferson as my favourite American President.[9] But for the most part suspicion reigned; and this

5. Max Beloff, *Foreign Policy and the Democratic Process* (Baltimore: 1955). Baltimore was an interesting city for me in another way. I got to know Hamilton Owens, the editor of the *Baltimore Sun*; and it was to the *Baltimore Sun* that the *Manchester Guardian* had transferred its title deeds in order to prevent a Nazi takeover of the title should Britain have been successfully invaded.
6. Max Beloff, *The United States and the Unity of Europe* (Washington, DC: 1963).
7. See Max Beloff, 'The Special Relationship: An Anglo-American Myth', in Martin Gilbert (ed.), *A Century of Conflict* (London: 1967), republished in Max Beloff, *The Intellectual in Politics and Other Essays* (London: 1970).
8. The Anglo-American relationship is dealt with at some length in Max Beloff, *Imperial Sunset*, vol. 1: *Britain's Liberal Empire, 1897–1921* (London: 1969; New York: 1970; 2nd edn, London: 1987; New York: 1988), and vol. 2: *Dream of Commonwealth, 1921–1942* (London: 1989; New York: 1989).
9. See the essays collected in Part II, 'America', of Max Beloff, *The Great Powers* (London: 1959) and in particular 'Theodore Roosevelt and the British Empire: A Centennial Lecture'. The comparison with Jefferson is not as odd as it might seem at first sight. Justice Felix Frankfurter told me that, of all the Presidents he had known during his long career, Theodore Roosevelt was the 'egghead' – not, be it noted, Professor Woodrow Wilson.

became more noticeable when ideologues of the Democratic Party were in the ascendant: Woodrow Wilson, Franklin Roosevelt. Even knowing the ultimate contribution that Roosevelt's America made to Hitler's defeat and Britain's salvation, one could not disguise the fact, which grows ever clearer as the wartime records become available, that the ending of the British Empire was seen by him as an inevitable and desirable outcome of the war. Similarly, Roosevelt's illusion that he could get along better with Stalin than Churchill could arose from his belief that his ideas on 'imperialism' were the same as the Soviet tyrant's. It is fair to add that the hostility of Roosevelt and his successors to 'imperialism' was not confined to issues affecting the British Empire; it helped to dictate Roosevelt's attitude to de Gaulle, for which NATO is still paying. The determination of the Americans to impede France's recovery of its pre-war position in Indo-China may have led to the later American involvement in Vietnam – in which case French 'imperialists' were most powerfully avenged. In any event I have continued to take the view that histories of the Anglo-American relationship which do not give emphasis to the imperial aspects of the matter are lacking in a vital respect.[10]

In the period of Cold War that followed the breakdown of the brief alignment between the United States and the Soviet Union over the pattern of future peace, the position of the United States as a non-imperialist power was challenged not merely by the Soviet Union itself – at least until its own empire began to crumble in the late 1980s – but also by the newly emancipated states that emerged from the debris of the British and other European overseas empires. And such accusations were readily voiced by Latin American countries, which although long independent in formal status felt themselves to be economically at the mercy of American capital.

American material civilization provided a model for imitation and assimilation by most of the rest of the world even, as was to become plain, in the communist-controlled world. But, at the same time, the institutions and ideology that had made these material achievements possible were repudiated. The United States, which had been the product of a successful revolution and

10. Max Beloff, 'The End of the British Empire and the Assumption of World-wide Commitments by the United States', in W. R. Louis and Hedley Bull (eds), *The 'Special Relationship'* (Oxford: 1986).

which still thought of itself as in the van of political and social progress, was widely seen as a reactionary force and the bulwark of regimes that openly repudiated its ideals. America has been made more difficult in a way unforeseen and unforeseeable by Tocqueville and other nineteenth-century prophets of the country's future. The difficulty for a democracy of pursuing a foreign policy and of making the sacrifices such a policy might demand has been compensated for in part by the ability to use modern means of mass communication to create a common perception of external threats that required joint action to avert. Such a perception was bound to be simplistic and often carried to excess. It was not always the safest guide to policy.

It has thus been the case not merely that the United States has had a self-image that does not correspond to how much of the world sees it but also that its internal political differences tend to be magnified by their involvement with external ideological conflicts. None of this is of course peculiar to the United States. Any country which for a variety of quite practical reasons desires to project its power and its influence abroad is likely to build up self-justifying bodies of doctrine of which its own innate superiority is one important element. This was true of the creation of the 'Second' largely Asian British Empire at the turn of the eighteenth and nineteenth centuries.[11] French, German and Russian parallels would not be hard to find. But the unwillingness of the United States (or its inability) to accept enlightened self-interest as sufficient to justify its external policies is both remarkable and a testimony to the hold over the American imagination of the original commitment to being different from the Old World.

It does, however, mean that the pursuit of foreign-policy objectives, particularly if unsuccessful, but even if it can simply be shown that the United States is not looked up to gratefully by its beneficiaries, can create major divisions domestically and can lead to renewed credence being given to George Washington's warning about foreign entanglements. It is understandable that a retreat into isolation should so frequently close a period of expansion; and here right and left – in so far as these terms are applicable in an American context – may find common ground.

11. For a recent examination of this theme, see C. A. Bayly, *Imperial Meridian: The British Empire and the World, 1780–1830* (London: 1989).

It is of course comforting to the historian to find that a country continues to act, as it were, in character. But one must be careful not to let this conclusion conceal the fact that the United States has been changing in a variety of ways that have an impact upon the conduct of its external relations. By and large the Americans occupy the same terrain as they have done for most of their history. But, if the physical geography is a constant, this is not true of the human geography in respect either of the composition of the population or of its distribution. The United States has at all times been a country of immigration. The make-up and scale of that immigration have differed widely between successive historical periods. Each wave of immigrants has left its mark and each has successively strained against the Anglocentric cultural and institutional heritage it discovered in place. Germans and Irish in the middle of the nineteenth century, east Europeans at the turn of the nineteenth and twentieth centuries, Hispanics and Asians in recent years – all have, sometimes for a limited period, sometimes more permanently, affected the American vision of the world. To these successive waves of newcomers must be added the descendants of those who were there almost from the beginning, slaves of African origin. Until their enfranchisement and the building up of a black leadership capable of playing a part in the American political process – and for that it was necessary to wait a good deal longer – they could not much affect the conduct of foreign policy. But they also have become a player in the game and have given it a bias of their own.

What actually happens depends, in individual cases, on how the organs of government operate and how the electoral system channels influence from those elements in the population who choose to be politically active. An analysis by numbers alone would not tell one much. Without understanding the provisions of the constitution or their early interpretation, one cannot grasp how American foreign policy is conducted, but it would be equally misleading to transpose what one finds into a contemporary setting. The leadership of the executive branch, that is to say the President, remains – enhanced maybe by his unique access to the media; the sole rights of Congress to declare war and of the Senate to ratify treaties also remain in place. And by and large this framework served well enough for the period up to the Second World War. Lessons could also be drawn from a failure to observe the implied preconditions of successful action, as when Woodrow Wilson failed to carry the Senate with him over the Treaty of

Versailles and the League of Nations. But the changes in the
extent and permanence of American overseas involvements, both
governmental and private, have altered the balance in favour of
Congress. A president now would know he would have to begin
by negotiating an agreement there.

Congress itself is not the body that it was. No senators retain
the independence of thought and action which was within living
memory the prerogative of at any rate a few. Congressmen never
made a similar individual impact, but today more than ever they
are in thrall to their voters, and to those who have financed them
for elections past and from whom they have hopes for elections
future. Their large staffs and spacious offices (which British MPs
misled by Americanophile dons so much admire) are symbols
not of independence but of their infeodation to special interests,
among which (for the present purpose) one must count the
representatives of ethnic groups. The prime object of the staffs is
to see that due attention is paid to the voices of whatever interest
or group may have votes or subsidies to offer. The congressman and even the senator has become a delegate rather than a
representative, in the sense of being unable to defy the elements
at home to which he is beholden.

While the electronic media may have helped the President they
have been harmful to senators and congressmen. Their cost is
such that only a very rich man could afford an election state-wide
every six years or district-wide every two years. So for most
candidates the money must come from others; they will not give it
without seeking some private advantage. To some extent this is
true of the President also, at least where securing the nomination
is concerned. The pressures in a nation-wide constituency may
partially cancel each other out, but the electoral system is such –
especially with the generalization of primaries – that powerful
interests in some states need to be taken fully into account.

It is not so much the individual ethnic origin or personal
inclination of an individual senator or congressman that may
affect his attitude towards individual problems in foreign policy, as
his estimate of what most of his constituents want or will accept.
Nor of course will the pressures upon him always be in the same
direction. He may be asked for reasons of principle or to permit a
lowering of taxes to push for greater measures of disarmament –
but what if his constituency has an important section depending
upon a military installation or the manufacture of armaments? He
may believe that free trade is the avenue to general prosperity in

the United States and in the world at large, but what if an industry in his constituency is clamouring for protection against alleged unfair competition from abroad? In coming to a conclusion he is likely to take into account the well-proved fact – and one not limited to the American scene – that those who fear damage to a special interest will make more fuss than those who are in favour of some more general objective.

What is to be noted is that while it is the impact of what is done upon other countries affected that will be uppermost in the minds of the executive branch – re-election considerations not withstanding – this aspect is not likely to be uppermost in the minds of legislators, except for a few who for one reason or another have carved out a recognized specialism in foreign affairs. Because of the way in which the constitutional relationships have developed and because of the absence for most purposes of the party discipline familiar to Europe, the individual American senator or congressman has much more power than his European counterpart; but he knows much less about the external world. Because of the uniqueness of the American experience and because the study of history – notably non-American history – has been downgraded in American education, including higher education, there is often a frightening lack of understanding by Americans of the world in which the United States has to operate, and in this ignorance they merely reflect their constituents. If I had to revise my earlier writings upon the United States I would need to take much of this into account.

The development of Congressional authority directly mirroring the pressures of the electorate is likely also to prove of significance in respect of an issue which did not often figure in public debate when I began my study of the United States half a century ago, and that is what is now generally referred to as the environment. It is true that under the label 'conservation' there had been some controversy over such matters earlier in the century, but it was not thought to have an international dimension. How and at what speed and by whom the natural resources of the United States should be exploited was a domestic question. Now that it has become part of a global concern, the domestic pressure on the US government not to sacrifice short-term considerations in pursuit of long-term international goals makes it a difficult partner in the search for solutions to world problems. For an inevitable characteristic of Congressional government is the elevation of the short term over the long.

The extreme emphasis given by American society to consumerism and the antipathy to regulation and state provision of a large majority of active citizens does explain many policies that would seem questionable to other countries where a more direct sense of the national interest has prevailed. No doubt this has its advantages in the elasticity that has continued to mark the American economy, but again it is something that would now bulk large in any study of the evolution of American institutions.

In some respects, the United States has continued to occupy a particular position among western democracies, as it was seen to do in the world at large by the Founding Fathers. Madison's belief that in a large country the danger that factional interests would make governance impossible or wholly partisan would be avoided because the interests would balance each other and thus force a consensus has proved correct. But the mechanism through which this would happen could not have been foreseen. The principal agent of reconciliation has been the party system: the tendency of parties to become the voices of particular groups and hence to multiply has been curtailed by the joint pressures of the separation of powers and of the electoral system. At both state and national level, the chief executive is a single person, so in the end most electoral contests end up as two-horse races. And where the legislatures are concerned, the new country's inheritance of a plurality system in single-member (or in the Senate two-member) constituencies saved the United States from the logically seductive but practically fatal temptations of proportional representation. Finally the need to produce every four years two plausible presidential candidates has overcome what might otherwise be the consequences of the very different connotations in different states and regions of the two principal parties, whose names and continuous existence go back to pre-Civil War times. No one need sacrifice much in material terms or in respect of principle by making this four-yearly gesture to unanimity. While in most western countries political parties are classified in terms of the interests or ideologies they represent – in many cases along the left–right divide established as we have seen by the French Revolution – in the United States the parties can provide labels for bottles of widely differing content over time and across the country.

It may be that this classical analysis is beginning to show signs of weakness. It may be that United States Democrats do correspond more and more to European social democrats and

Republicans to European Liberal–Conservatives, but the analogy
is never likely to be complete. The fact that for so much of the
last forty years we have seen the presidency when held by the
Republicans more often than not facing a Democratic majority in
one or both Houses of Congress is worth noting as something I
could not have foreseen when writing on the American federal
government in the late 1950s. For this experience carries with it
two conclusions about the American political system. It suggests
that large numbers of voters find it easy to cross party lines when
it comes to voting for a presidential candidate. It also suggests a
degree of consensus across the political spectrum which makes it
possible for a system of separation of powers to operate without
deadlock. Such co-operation would not necessarily be impossible
in Europe; we have the example of 'co-habitation' when the
socialist President of France, François Mitterrand, had to get
along with a right-wing prime minister and cabinet. But one has
only to translate this into British terms to see how different is the
American party scene. Where such difference in political control
exists, it does of course make the carrying through of a radical
legislative programme much more difficult. On the other hand,
such programmes – the Roosevelt New Deal for instance – are
anyhow rare in the American context. While party leaders in
Britain enter upon general election campaigns with a manifesto
containing a list of legislative proposals for which if victorious
they claim a 'mandate', American presidential candidates having
to appeal to so diverse an electorate normally do their best to
avoid precise commitments.

It was less difficult writing in the 1950s after *Brown* v. *Topeka*
to overlook the possibility of another period of judicial activism
and hence of the continued politicization of the American judiciary. This attitude to the judiciary as being not simply the final
authority for the interpretation of the constitution and hence of
the constitutionality of federal and state legislation but part of the
legislative apparatus itself had made vast strides when I gave a few
lectures in the United States during the widespread celebration of
the bicentennial of the constitution. Powerful pressure groups
have shown a determination to use their hold over Congress and
to a lesser extent the presidency to secure nominations to the
Supreme Court that appear likely to forward their particular aims.
It can be argued that this has always been the case, and that
American constitutional history has always had to concern itself
with court decisions to a much greater degree than the con-

stitutional history of other democratic governments. But there did seem to me in the 1980s an almost cynical indifference to the ultimate impact of judicial activism and to the difficulty of forcing out of an eighteenth-century document answers to questions that would not have occurred, in some cases could not have occurred, to its makers.

Such an attitude might be expected of the pressure groups themselves and of politicians eager to curry favour with them, but it was a shock to discover how often this indifference to the distinction between constitutional argument and sheer prejudice had crept into the academy itself. One opens a book entitled *Foundations of American Constitutionalism* by a professor of law at a well-known university.[12] The author parades much learning in an investigation of the intellectual background and historical inheritance of the Founding Fathers. It is only as one reads his book that one becomes aware that nothing could be further from the author's intention than to explain the meaning of the con-stitution in such terms. The work is on the contrary a disguised polemic justifying the conduct of those who successfully thwarted the nomination to the Supreme Court of Robert Bork because it was felt by the feminist pro-abortion lobby that his 'strict constructionist' approach to the constitution might lead him to side with those who held that the issues raised by such questions should be regulated by the state legislatures rather than by a remote, non-elected federal judiciary. I was in the United States while the Senate hearings on the Bork nomination were in pro-cess, and I was struck by the total indifference of Bork's opponents to any question of his general suitability in terms of legal training or character for a place on the court. While it was the feminist lobby that made the running, its protagonists did not hesitate to try to enlist, in part successfully, assistance from leaders of the black community with accusations (for which no evidence was produced) that Bork was not only a 'strict constructionist' but also a 'racist'.

It has been inevitable in a country ultimately governed accord-ing to a written constitution now over 200 years old, with in-built obstacles to its amendment, that the courts as its interpreters should have played so important a role. While this is most

---

12. David A. J. Richards, *Foundations of American Constitutionalism* (New York: 1989).

obviously true in the sphere of race relations, where some court decisions clearly helped precipitate the Civil War and to retard the progress of ex-slaves and their descendants to full legal equality, other aspects of national policy have also been determined as to the pace and shape of change by the need to take account of the constitutional aspects of proposed governmental action. It could be argued that what was affected was the speed of change rather than its nature. The regulation of the economy, progressive taxation, welfare provision – all have come to exist in the United States as in other advanced industrial countries. Such differences as exist are due more to the nature of American society than to the constitutional constraints upon governmental action.

It would be interesting to reflect on the impact of such experience on the Anglo-American dialogue, particularly since the legal profession is the one with the most cross-Atlantic ties. While the universities in the United States saw in the late nineteenth century an eclipse of the original English and Scottish inheritance by German models, the American legal system remained close to its common law origins.[13] Where British academics and other commentators on the American scene are concerned, one has to reckon that most of those interested in America have at least until recently been politically left of centre. On the whole therefore British comment tended to side with Franklin Roosevelt in his impatience with what he saw as Supreme Court obstruction to the New Deal. On the other hand there was much sympathy with the court when it began in a new phase of judicial activism to demolish much of the legacy of racial discrimination. Whether British academics will be so enthusiastic when they come to appreciate the highly damaging impact of 'affirmative action' upon the American universities (whether exercised in favour of women or of racial minorities) is a subject for speculation. But they may conclude that once again it is society, not the legislators nor the courts, that is to blame. The tendency to a uniformity of attitudes long observed in American society remains particularly true of its intellectual component University presidents and professors have

13.   It is notable, however, that when the reform of the British legal system was being debated during the passage in 1989–90 of the Courts and Legal Services Bill the Lord Chancellor refused to take account of the warnings of US lawyers against importing into the British system some of the worst abuses of American practice. It is a pity when there is a 'special relationship' not to make use of it.

repeatedly shown themselves all too prone to accept at face value the demands of revolting students or of radical chic. The craggy individualists who were often the glory of American academe a generation ago are now hard to find.

In the last few years another possible rapprochement between the British and American systems of government has been talked about in Britain. Voices have been raised in Britain to bemoan the alleged lack of human rights and the alleged absolutism of elected governments. The answer, it is said, is for Britain to have a written constitution and a Bill of Rights. It is true that much of the American constitution, being one for a federation, would not be easily transferable into British circumstances, and that the model for a Bill of Rights is sought in continental Europe rather than North America. Indeed the most usual suggestion is that the European Convention on Human Rights should be incorporated into British domestic law.

Nevertheless it is the United States that has the longest experience of a written constitution to which we have access, and it is curious that so little attention has been paid to its manifest disadvantages, or to the small extent to which the principle of Parliamentary sovereignty can be combined with an increasingly political role for the judiciary. No doubt more attention is paid to history in Britain than in the United States, and more to American history itself than when I began teaching the subject half a century ago. But there seems a regrettable willingness to argue that any practice prevalent in the United States is suitable for imitation in this country. And this is not only a question of political institutions. In education foolish American theories were taken over wholesale in the 1960's and, while the United States is now trying to shake off their effects, they still impede in this country the necessary process of educational reform.[14]

14.  The borrowing of an American vocabulary is both symptomatic and perilous. When I went to university I had been a schoolboy or pupil and became an undergraduate. Now everyone being educated at almost any age is called a 'student' or, worse still, a 'kid', which is held to absolve him or her from intellectual or moral responsibility, and teachers from trying to inculcate the discipline upon which intellectual achievement depends.

# V

# The Russian Enigma: In or Out?

A German general of the First World War wrote a book entitled *Der Krieg der Versäumten Gelegenheiten*, 'The War of Lost Opportunities'. The title has stuck with me. It comes back when I consider my brief incursion into Russian history. Why did I not use the occasion to make Russian history my central interest? In part this was due to the accidental nature of my first contact with the subject, to which I have referred in the Introduction. My own work for Chatham House expanded into a two-volume history of Soviet foreign policy between 1929 and Hitler's assault upon the Soviet Union in June 1941.[1] Again the choice of where to begin was based not upon any clear perception of the periods into which the subject might be usefully divided, but upon the fact that the only large-scale study available, by the American journalist Louis Fischer, ended in 1929.

My own work was very different from Fischer's. Not merely did he have the advantage of having spent some time in the Soviet Union and of having had a personal acquaintance with some of its leading figures before the Stalinist night descended and made such contacts dangerous, but he was also touched by the idealism with which many in the west greeted the Revolution in its early stages. I had no access to any but printed sources, most of them non-Russian, though I got some help from individuals who had been associated with negotiations between the United Kingdom and the Soviet Union. I was also not inspired by any particular

---

1. Max Beloff, *The Foreign Policy of Soviet Russia, 1929–41*, 2 vols (London: 1947, 1949).

sympathy with the Soviet government or its conduct, and tried to deal with the subject with the same degree of distance and objectivity as my historical training in another field had inculcated.

As the problems of handling Soviet policy in the post-war period began to reveal themselves, Chatham House also asked me to undertake a study of their Far Eastern aspect, and this duly appeared a few years later.[2] While *The Foreign Policy of Soviet Russia* remained essential reading for students for quite a number of years – I used to meet US servicemen who had been made to read it at their war colleges – the Far Eastern book was much less satisfactory. The material was harder to acquire; my knowledge of East Asia was too elementary; and I had by then begun to feel more wedded to my American interests.

It was reasonable at the time to feel that the study of an open society was preferable to dealing with one that seemed hermetically sealed and likely to remain so. One could with the aid of personal contacts find one's way around the many profound differences of opinion that enveloped important aspects of the American past. Soviet historians seemed mere voices for the current orthodoxies, behind which it was hard for a foreigner to penetrate. It was of course possible to accept these limitations and write Soviet history on the basis of what documents the Soviet authorities were prepared to publish, as did E. H. Carr, but to try to get a rounded view seemed then an almost impossible task. It was not until the 1980s that circumstances changed to the extent that Soviet studies could be resumed as an exciting and intellectually rewarding field of academic activity.

What I do regard as a possibly lost opportunity was not having done something to master not Soviet but pre-Soviet history, at least from the rich printed sources available in the west. I made a beginning by looking at eighteenth-century Russia to meet an invitation to contribute to a book on the nobility of the period. But that was all.[3]

Yet this did not mean that I was oblivious to the need for understanding the Russian basis of the Soviet state, nor to the principal differences that colour interpretations of that relationship. The one that was given new prominence in the Gorbachev

---

2. Max Beloff, *Soviet Policy in the Far East, 1944–51* (London: 1953).
3. Max Beloff, 'Russia', in A. Goodwin (ed.), *The European Nobility in the Eighteenth Century* (London: 1953).

era is whether Russian history is indeed part of European history
or whether it has always been apart so that Russia cannot be
encompassed in one's view of Europe or fitted into any common
institutions that Europe may develop.

I do not think myself that I ever accepted Russia as not being
part of Europe, or ever regarded the Revolution of 1917 as other
than an interruption of the development that Russia would have
followed alongside that of the other European powers with whom
its fortunes had been linked since the sixteenth century. The issue
first presented itself to me when studying the early phases of
European integration in the 1940s and 1950s, entered upon by
western nations and regarded with unconcealed animosity by the
Soviet government. In an essay on this topic, I quoted with
approval the words of the most learned of British historians of
Russia at the time, B. H. Sumner:

> The choice must be made between regarding Russia either as
> a world to herself or as in the main belonging to Europe. On
> the whole I should say that the new Europe, which took such a
> variety of shapes in the eighteenth and nineteenth century, was
> in such continuous and close contact with Russia that by 1900
> Russia was perhaps more European than at any other time in
> her history.

And I supported, as against Arnold Toynbee's view that Russia
was permanently divided from Europe because of its Orthodox
rather than Roman Catholic inheritance, the view of Professor
Dmitri Obolensky that Byzantium had been a link between Russia
and the rest of Europe, not the source of its separation.[4]

To take this view was of course to resist the argument that the
Soviet system was in some sense a natural outgrowth of Russia's
past and to see it rather as a destructive irruption consisting of the
capture of the state by an ideologically inspired conspiracy with its
outcome perpetuated by a self-interested and self-blinkered ruling
stratum. Such a view explains why, when I came to review the
history of Russia in the nineteenth century by Sumner's successor
as the doyen of British historians of Russia, I headed my review
'Before the Flood'.[5] That is not to say that there were no respects

4.   Max Beloff, 'The Russian View of European Integration', reprinted from *The
European Yearbook* (1956) in Max Beloff, *The Great Powers* (London: 1959).

5.   Max Beloff, 'Before the Flood', a review of Hugh Seton-Watson, *The Russian
Empire, 1801–1917*, reprinted from *Encounter* in Max Beloff, *The Intellectual
in Politics and other Essays* (London: 1970).

in which Russia's previous institutions and the cast of mind they engendered did not make the communist appeal particularly hard to resist – the elevation of the state, the impatience with legal norms as against the ill-defined concept of 'justice' – but without the war and the opportunity it provided for Lenin the patchy progress, economic and social, of Tsarism's final decades might have had a more propitious outcome.

In any event, the idea that there was now no important gap between the Soviet Union and the rest of the advanced industrial world and the theories of 'convergence' that once flourished seemed to me quite untenable. My one and only (brief) visit to the Soviet Union merely confirmed that belief.[6]

One reason for such differences of opinion may lie in the exaggerated emphasis upon economic, political and legal aspects of the problem by those who maintain the doctrine of Russia's separation. Of course these aspects are important; the possibility of a fully civilized life depends upon how they are tackled, as the history of the Soviet Union itself exemplifies. But they are not decisive. One has only to think of what European cultural experience from 1815 to 1917 would look and sound like if the Russian contribution were removed.

Can one seriously maintain that Turgenev, Dostoevsky and Tolstoy are not part of the mainstream of European literature, even if Russian lyrical poetry is difficult to appreciate in another idiom? Can one study the development of modern drama without acknowledging the influence of Chekhov? Above all there is music. It is true that Russian music bears a strong national imprint. But it is as part of European music that it falls to be considered; one has only to compare it with Indian music for example, to say nothing of the African rhythms so congenial to today's youth, to see that this is so. Once again, it is hard to imagine European music without Tchaikovsky, Rimsky-Korsakov, Rachmaninov, Prokofiev, Stravinsky. And if one holds, as I do, that opera is the art form in which the European spirit reached its peak, are there three operas so redolent of the history of their country and at the same time so central to European operatic experience as *Prince Igor*, *Khovantschina* and *Boris Godunov*?

It is also worth remembering the enormous impact made in theatrical as well as musical representation by the flowering of the

6.   Max Beloff, 'Soviet Studies and Russian Reality', *The Times*, 22 September 1965, reprinted in *The Intellectual in Politics*.

Russian stage in the last years of Tsarism – the methods of the Moscow Art Theatre and the example of the Russian ballet were vital elements in the European culture of the period. And Russian singers and instrumentalists were fêted in western Europe (as well as America) before the Revolution and, in the case of its survivors, after it.

A recent study of the Russian ruling class in the last decades of Tsarism has pointed out that here was:

> a state which treated its subjects in a more arbitrary and at times brutal manner than was true of any of the other major European states . . . yet here too was a traditional upper class whose nineteenth-century contributions in the fields of literature and music were far more impressive than those of any of their European peers.[7]

One must also remember that there was direct interaction between the Russian intelligentsia and that of the west. The form taken by the Tsarist repression was conducive to exile, and exile in turn conducive to vigorous cultural life, which left at least some mark on the host countries, however closely the exiles might cling together.[8]

Anti-semitic pressures in the later phase of Tsarism produced a further large-scale migration, most but not all of it non-political. Brought up in a household with these antecedents and used to hearing Russian as an everyday instrument of communication between my parents and their friends, as well as conscious of the role that music played in the lives of the exiled community, and with some contacts with its Parisian counterpart, I am perhaps especially sensitive to this aspect of Russia's links with Europe. The Revolution itself and the vicissitudes of the Soviet Union until today have produced successive waves of émigrés carrying with them in many cases and for more than one generation some imprint of their origin.[9]

7.  Dominic Lieven, *Russia's Rulers under the Old Regime* (New Haven and London: 1989), p. 206.
8.  Since I am critical of E. H. Carr's main historical works, I would like pay tribute to his pioneer study of Herzen and his circle in *The Romantic Exiles: A Nineteenth Century Portrait Gallery* (London: 1933).
9.  For a recent and moving collection of the oral testimonies of émigrés, see Norman Stone and Michael Glenny (eds), *The Other Russia* (London: 1990).

What has been true of each successive wave of the politically minded émigrés was their insistence on their own interpretation of what had gone wrong. This was particularly true of the Russians who left during or immediately after the Revolution and who in exile turned their old debates on what should be done into debates on what should have been done. Emigration also affected the thinking of individuals about the history of Russia over a much longer period. Historians among the post-1917 turned to such long-range speculation rather than to the painful survey of the Revolution and its aftermath.[10] They were influenced in their approach by their experience in the universities of the late Tsarist period and by the difficult course they had to follow between the demands of the state which was their paymaster and the radical wave then sweeping over the country.[11]

For a lively cultural life, for the preservation of Russian sentiments and for the creation of communal institutions, some geographical concentration was required. Parts of the post-revolutionary emigration remained in other Slavonic countries in Europe – notably in Czechoslovakia and Yugoslavia – the former providing largely for those of a democratic disposition, the latter for the hard right, political and ecclesiastical. Other members of the emigration found themselves in the Far East, notably in Harbin and Shanghai. Some moved directly on to the Americas. But, between the Revolution and the Second World War, two cities were the main centres of Russian activity in exile – Berlin and Paris. London, a less important centre for Russians and other exiles than in the nineteenth century, was to some extent subordinate to ideas and personalities in both these major centres.

Berlin was for many reasons the first important centre of the migration: ties with Germany had existed for many of the immigrants and were now renewed.[12] But it proved for many Russians only a temporary stopping-place. For those with some

10. The dilemmas and achievements of the historians in exile are fully canvassed in Marc Rueff, *Russia Abroad: A Cultural History of the Russian Emigration, 1919– 39* (New York: 1990).

11. The subject is treated in detail with due attention to the impact of developments elsewhere, particularly in Germany, in Samuel D. Kassov, *Students, Professors and the State in Tsarist Russia* (Berkeley: California, 1990).

12. See Robert C. Williams, *Culture in Exile: Russian Emigrés in Germany, 1881–1941* (Ithaca, NY, and London: 1972).

assets, Germany in the early years of the Weimar Republic was a cheap place to live. With the stabilization of the currency, it became more expensive, and Paris proved the greater attraction. Furthermore the difficulties placed upon émigré political activity in Germany in the 1930s made it a less appropriate centre for the exiles' leadership.

From the mid-1920s to the fall of France, it was Paris that saw the main efflorescence of Russian émigré cultural institutions, the long-drawn-out arguments about the reasons for the Soviet triumph, and the consequent search for a political formula for what was to follow the constantly anticipated disappearance of the Soviet regime.[13] Those faithful to Tsarism received little leadership or guidance from the representatives abroad of the Romanov dynasty. Much energy was spent in countering the activities of Soviet agents. Of more intellectual interest were the divisions on the socialist non-communist left between the Mensheviks and the Social Revolutionaries and between those Constitutional Democrats like V. A. Maklakov who wished to hold on to the total independence of the party and those like the historian and former minister in the provisional government, Paul Milioukov, who sought in exile an opening to the left.

Even more fundamental was the question whether the Soviet regime itself might evolve to a point when there could be a reconciliation with the Russian emigration. Some émigrés returned home, with disastrous consequences for most of them. By and large however, almost all the factions within the émigré world fought against the initial recognition of the Soviet government by their host countries and, after this had become general, endeavoured to expose the realities of the Soviet regime against the often over-optimistic accounts current in the west. In that sense of course they were following the example of earlier generations of Russian exiles who had called attention to the misdeeds of Tsarism. The battle of images was to be renewed in the years after the Second World War. It was only in the 1980s that official revelations in the Soviet Union itself finally made nonsense of the optimistic picture given by the Webbs and their successors.

For the earlier generation a new issue of conscience had arisen with the advent of Hitler and the growing threat to the Soviet Union's very existence. In the event, Hitler did manage to recruit

13.　See Robert H. Johnston, *New Mecca – New Babylon: Paris and the Russian Exiles, 1920–45* (Kingston and Montreal: 1988).

some Russians to his banner, but most of the emigration in France remained faithful to their new homeland, and after 1940 some of its members took part in the Resistance. For a brief moment after the Liberation the prospects of reconciliation with the Soviet regime seemed to brighten. On 12 February 1945, Maklakov attended a reception at the Soviet Embassy in the very building where he himself had been ambassador in 1917. Events both inside and outside the Soviet Union soon made such hopes unrealistic, and the subsequent history of the Russian emigration, centred as it was in New York, is part of the history of the Cold War.

Recent studies of the earlier emigration seem to me in the light of my own memories and knowledge to have underplayed the role of a specifically Jewish element. Professor Johnston for instance pays no attention to the important role in the early years of the Paris emigration of Maxim Vinaver, a Jewish member of the first Duma and a powerful advocate of Jewish rights in the last decades of Tsarism.[14] Until his death in 1926 he was concerned among other matters with repudiating the right-wing allegations that the Revolution had been the work of an international Jewish conspiracy. One reason for this omission of the Jewish element may be that Johnston (like Robert Williams and Marc Rueff) tends to see Russian culture among the émigrés, which is his main interest, in terms of the Orthodox Church and its related institutions. Given the importance to Russian cultural history of the Church both in music and in the visual arts and its contribution to some philosophical positions, such a concentration is perhaps understandable. But this does not cover the entire spectrum of the emigration or of its activities. It is in the Jewish case that one finds the greatest continuity between post-1917 emigration and its predecessors. As this is a notable aspect of the history of Zionism, I shall return to it in that aspect in the next chapter.

From quite a different angle there is a particular significance in the fortunes of the Russian emigration in Paris, particularly in its scholarly component. France and the French Revolution had bulked large in the interpretation of events in Russia from both Marxist and non-Marxist quarters.[15] Russia could no more than any other European country escape the impact of the French

14.  See P. E. Milioukov et al., M. M. Vinaver i Russkaya Obschestvennost Nachala XX Veka (Paris: 1937).
15.  Alain Besançon, 'La Russie et la Révolution française', in F. Furet and M. Ozouf eds). The Transformation of Political Culture, 1789–1948 (Oxford: 1989).

Revolution; what was specific about its experience was the fact that the timetable of social evolution was so different. Russia was only just entering the phase of enlightened despotism when the Revolution and its ideas burst upon it; in much of the rest of Europe the ground had to some extent been prepared. While the use of the French language by the Russian upper class made French ideas particularly accessible, this influence later declined in favour of that of the German ideas critical of the French legacy, whether nationalism with a particular theocratic slant or socialism. So, when Nicholas I died and the way was open for the feverish period of reform under Alexander II, French ideas were in eclipse. But the spread of industry and education gave new verisimilitude to the French Revolution model.

The record of the French Revolution was both an inspiration and a warning. The ending of serfdom in Russia had not fully emancipated the peasantry, who were still legally and politically separate from the rest of society. Not until the turn of the century did the peasants begin to receive an education. Until illiteracy had been conquered and the peasants had been brought into the general legal and social framework, the liberal elements in the intelligentsia feared their irruption on to the political scene, while having to avoid being outflanked on the left by parties with no such fears. It proved impossible in the time available before the war, and in the face of widespread allegiance to earlier ideas, to parallel the French progress towards the creation of a bourgeois society. The revolutionary groups indifferent to such processes used direct action to stimulate reaction and hence to popularize themselves. Whether, had there been peace, there might have been such an evolution is a matter only for speculation. Given the pace of Russian economic expansion, and the expansion of popular education, both long overlooked by those who believed in the realities of Soviet construction, it cannot be ruled out. What happened, as we know, was very different and wholly tragic. As a leading French authority on these matters has written:

> La guerre de 1914 en détruisant l'Etat, en ruinant la Société, en desorganisant les partis populaires et social democrates, donna sa chance à Lenine qui sut la saisir. La Révolution russe qui depuis 1905 semblait suivre, pas à pas, les étapes classiques de la révolution anglaise et française, soudain bifurqua dans une direction inconnue et passa de l'autre côté du mirroir. [16]

16.   *Ibid.*, p. 582.

The rapid and confused changes that have taken place in the former Soviet Union over the last few years have seen western historians and social scientists trying to keep up with them in their interpretations and trying to bring the past to their aid, particularly since a rediscovery of their own past is one of the ways in which Russians themselves are now seeking to establish their own identity. Sometimes these echoes can be awe-inspiring in their impact. Gorbachev's *perestroika* and *glasnost* involved a stream of new laws and governmental directives. Yet such was the resistance of the existing structure of political and social authority that it has never been clear how far what was commanded from the centre was actually put into effect. The correspondence of radical reformers in the early part of the reign of Alexander II constantly illuminates this same contradiction. The Russians can see what a better society would look like but find it hard to take the steps necessary to get there.[17]

Even more remarkable is the parallel between the Stalinist era and the picture of Russia that had been the product of the reaction under Nicholas I after the crushing of the Decembrist revolt in 1825. This picture was fostered in the west by the writings of those who, like Herzen, had contrived to find a way out of Russia. In particular the Polish emigration after the failed rising of 1830–1 was always present to prevent anyone forgetting that Russia was a prison-house of peoples. The degree to which Nicholas's regime rested upon Orthodoxy here highlighted the ancient religious divide between Catholic and Orthodox Europe.

In the era of the industrial revolution, the existence of an economy still based upon the personal servitude of the mass of the population was itself a constant challenge to the observer from abroad. The legalized class structure, almost extending to a caste system, was constantly under observation in relation to a governmental apparatus in which there was an overlap between its civil and military elements to an extent unfamiliar in the west. The lack of a recognized rule of law binding upon the ruler himself, the rigidity of the censorship and the ubiquity of the political police – all these struck the foreign visitor and the thinking Russian alike.[18]

17. See Franco Venturi, *Roots of Revolution* (London: 1960).
18. Among Russian exiled writers on the subject, I. Golovine attracted attention for his *Russia under the Autocrat Nicholas I* (London: 1846), reviewed in the *Athenaeum*, 14 March 1846. Golovine was the subject of a very hostile description by Herzen. See Alexander Herzen, *My Past and Thoughts: The*

It is not surprising that in the age of the Cold War earlier descriptions of Russia stressing these elements should have found a ready readership.[19] And, when it was discovered belatedly how dependent the Soviet economic system was upon the evasion of formal regulations and upon bribery as the only lubricant, the same texts could be read again in a new light.

Russian critics of the regime of Nicholas I felt above all that everything was being sacrificed to the build-up of military power required both to maintain the empire in being and to furnish troops for further expansion, at this time mainly in the Caucasus. Is our mission, asked the spokesman of Russian populism, Chernyshevsky:

> to be omnipotent from the military point of view, and nothing as regards any other, superior aspect of national life? In that case it would be better not to have been born at all than to be born a Russian, as it would have been better not to have been born than to have been born a Hun, Attila, Genghis Khan, Tamburlaine, or one of their warriors and subjects.[20]

It was on this aspect that most British attention was likely to be focused. In general, the British were bound to be curious about an empire with which they had themselves had close commercial relations since the Elizabethan Age. Now they believed they were threatened by its pressure upon the fringes of the Indian Empire.[21] This dual interest, strategic and commercial, explains the form taken by a remarkable specimen of such literature, *Revelations of Russia*, described as by an 'English Resident' and published in

*Memoirs of Alexander Herzen*, trans. C. Garnett, rev. H. Higgens, 4 vols (London: 1968), vol. 3, pp. 1347–1418.

19.   The most celebrated foreign account was that by the Marquis de Custine, *La Russie en 1839*. An abbreviated translation with a very Cold War title, *A Journey for Our Times*, and with a preface by General W. Bedell Smith, the former US Ambassador in Moscow, was published in London in 1951. The controversy that Custine's work excited in France was closely followed in Britain. See *Quarterly Review*, CXLVI (March 1844) and *Edinburgh Review*, LX (April 1844).

20.   Quoted in Venturi, *Roots of Revolution*, p. 136.

21.   For most of the nineteenth century as the Russian Empire expanded over central Asia a struggle for influence persisted, with rival intelligence agents as well as more formal instruments of government playing a full part. See Peter Hopkirk, *The Great Game: Secret Service in High Asia* (Oxford: 1990), for a dramatic account of this aspect.

1844. The writer was clearly familiar with the work of Custine and other foreign observers and his depiction of the lineaments of the autocracy does not differ much from what others had written. He goes more deeply into the economic aspects of his subject and gives vivid illustrations of an economy held back by the perpetuation of serfdom, the lack of technological education and the absence of entrepreneurship.

Even more striking in the light of what we have recently discovered about the Soviet Union is this author's reference to statistics. He was writing at a time when statistical argument was very fashionable and he did his best with the figures for demography, trade and production. But, as with Russian statistics today, the figures could not be guaranteed to correspond with reality, whether by design or through sheer ignorance:

> All statistical accounts of Russia [he writes], like every other species of official reports, are little to be trusted, and returns of the population less than any; each document has to flow through so many channels, that it is more than probable that in one or other some interest at variance with the truth will cause it to be at once mutilated in the unscrupulous hands through which it passes.[22]

Quite apart from such wilful distortions there was in the bureaucracy an indifference to what the figures indicated; the important thing was that they should somehow be furnished.

Alexander Herzen, exiled to Vyatka and obliged to work in the Governor's office, provides us with an excellent example of what was amiss:

> The Ministry of Home Affairs had at that time [1838] a craze for statistics. It had given orders for committees to be formed everywhere and had issued programmes which could hardly be carried out but in Belgium or Switzerland; at the same time there were all sorts of tables with maxima and minima, with averages and totals for periods of ten years (made up of evidence which had not been collected for a year before) with moral remarks and metereological observations. Not a farthing was to be assigned for the expenses of the committees and the collection of evidence; all this was to be done from love of statistics

22. *Revelations of Russia, or The Emperor Nicholas and His Empire in 1844* by an English Resident (2nd edn, London: 1845), vol. 1, p. 364.

through the rural police and put into shape in the governor's office.[23]

*Revelations of Russia* was even more concerned with setting out the facts about Russian military strength and in pressing home the moral that Britain should embark upon a pre-emptive war before it became too overwhelming. A review of the work remarked that 'it strongly claims and will no doubt receive the eager and deep attention of this country'. On the other hand, the actual strength of Russia could be less threateningly assessed. The reviewer continues with an account from the manuscript notes of a 'recent traveller in Russia' of the military position which concludes that 'the military power of Russia is not so formidable as it is generally deemed in England and France and it may be fairly concluded that there is something radically vicious and defective in the military organization of Russia'.[24]

In the opinion of the reviewer the cardinal fault of *Revelations of Russia* was the anonymity of the authorship, which would detract from its utility. It would be claimed as the work of an exiled Pole or a dismissed official. Such a rebuke did not prevent the same writer publishing anonymously again a three-volume work the following year entitled *Eastern Europe and the Emperor Nicholas*.[25] In the preface to that work, the author warns against assuming from his earlier work that he cherished an anti-Russian prejudice. On the contrary, he had nothing but admiration and respect for the Russian people: 'Nothing could be more unjust than this confusion of victims and oppressor.' It is this confusion that he attributes to Custine and another recent French writer, Lacroix. What he now foresaw were convulsions in eastern Europe in which Britain might be called upon to intervene in unforeseeable ways. He drew a contrast between the contiguous democracies of western Europe and the four eastern imperial peoples: Germans, Russians, Austrians and Turks who ruled over multinational empires of Slavs, Finns, Magyars, Greeks and Albanians. Russia, he admits, had once roused the national feelings of the Slavs but they had now turned against it because of the experience of its iron rule. Of the empires, the Turks were the least oppressive and

23. Herzen, *My Past and Thoughts*, vol. 1, p. 232.
24. *Foreign Quarterly Review*, XXXIV (1845), pp. 194–200.
25. *Eastern Europe and the Emperor Nicholas* by the author of *Revelations of Russia* and *The White Slave*, 3 vols (London: 1946).

might well find allies among rebels against their Russo-German oppressors.[26] It is clear that the degree to which German influences predominated at the Russian court was a matter of common knowledge.

The writer claims that despite the censorship there was an interest among the Russians in what was written about them outside. He refers to a letter in the *Athenaeum* to the effect that a copy of *Revelations about Russia* had been bought for 500 roubles (£22) in St Petersburg and claims that 200 copies of the book had been smuggled in via Tiflis (Tbilisi).[27] The awakening of oppressed nationalities stimulated by the growth of the press across Europe is of great potential importance. Important too was the growth in national consciousness among 'Ruthenians', by whcich he signifies Little Russians or Ukrainians. But in such national movements there may be ambiguities: 'The revival of an extinct nationality is necesarily full of significance, though more often so puerile and unimportant as even to be encouraged by an ambitious government in its own dominions.' For instance the Russians were encouraging Finnish national sentiment, to weaken the hold of Finland's Swedish upper class and the consequent pull towards Sweden. Again the contemporary echoes are striking.

The main thrust remains the criticism of the regime and its social foundation. It is wrong to call the Russians serfs; they could more appropriately be styled slaves like the American negroes. The Russian autocrat wished to weaken the nobility by emancipating their serfs but was simultaneously adding to the number of his own. Tsardom was no longer as in an earlier period a vehicle for enlightenment. It was only misgovernment that kept the Russians poor.

This second work is very largely taken up with Poland and includes a detailed description of the Polish emigration, particularly in France with its various factions and leaders who between them maintained no fewer than eleven newspapers as well as two libraries. In volume three, a chapter is given over to Prussia's connivance with Russia in the suppression of the Poles and enters a plea for intervention on their behalf. The author

---

26.  The pro-Turkish slant prefigures that of an even more determined propagandist against Russia in the next generation, David Urquhart (1805–77), who assailed Palmerston for his alleged pro-Russian inclinations.
27.  *Athenaeum*, 12 April 1845.

detects a rapprochement between Nicholas I and Louis Philippe and was indeed within a couple of years to be publishing a new pamphlet arguing that Britain must maintain its defences so as to deter a possible French invasion.

Once one has penetrated the anonymity of the author of *Revelations of Russia* some things about his works become easier to explain. The description 'a resident in Russia' is misleading. He was in fact Charles Henningsen, who was born in London (or possibly in Belgium) of Swedish parents in 1815.[28] His family was established in London by 1830 and he was by then at any rate a British citizen. He saw service with the Spanish Carlists in 1835–6, of which he published an account in 1836. He took part in the anti-Russian military campaign of the Caucasian leader Schamyl and, after one of his defeats, became fugitive in Turkey. He was presumably in England during the period of intense literary activity which included his three-volume novel *The White Slave*. In the Hungarian rising of 1848 he distinguished himself in the field and, after the defeat of the rising, followed Kossuth into exile in Turkey and then to the United States, serving him as a confidential secretary. In 1856, he took part in William Walker's filibustering expedition to Nicaragua. Despite his anti-slavery sentiments, he later served in the Confederate Army. He died in Washington in 1877.[29]

It may seem odd to have spent so much time tracking down and chronicling the opinions of a not very successful soldier of fortune. But the tale has, I think, three morals.

In the first place, accounts of foreign countries and their institutions are not to be taken at face value. I do not know how much time Henningsen spent in Russia before he joined the Caucasian rebels. His information about the empire must have been gleaned before then, and one would like to know from whom. While his general political slant is clear, what particular causes he was representing is less so. Other writers must be subject to equally close scrutiny.

28.   Henningsen's Swedish antecedents may explain the somewhat incongruous attention he paid to disputing the Germanic origins of the English, so much stressed among Whig historians. Links with the Scandinavian peoples had been in his view far more important. *Eastern Europe and the Emperor Nicholas*, vol. 2, p. 217.

29.   *Appleton's American Biography*, vol. 3, 1889; *Dictionary of American Biography*, vol. 8. F. Boase (ed.), *Modern English Biography*, vol. 1 (Reprinted 1965).

Secondly, Henningsen's career is yet another reminder of how international a world was that of mid-nineteenth-century Europe. One thinks too easily in national compartmental terms; yet the rebels against the status quo – like the societies against which they were rebelling – had many links, not least for the rebels a common place of exile. Not only Russians and Poles, but Hungarians, Italians and Germans are the subject of Herzen's marvellous pen-pictures of their doings in mid-Victorian London, and of the material and moral difficulties that foreshadowed the fate of later generations of exiles. Subsequent events have given Marx and Engels, Lenin and Trotsky a special significance, but there is a wider and earlier context that needs to be taken into account.

Finally, it is important to indicate yet again that it was not only in quite recent times that questions of a country's internal regime have affected its relations with other countries. States are never able to act simply as *raison d'état* dictates, if only because there would be groups among their own people or among exiles who could be relied upon to put the contrary view. I first explored this element in international relations some thirty years ago when I looked at the role that a Jewish journalist, Lucien Wolf, played in stimulating and co-ordinating the Liberal and Labour pressure against the Asquith government's policy of seeking friendship with Tsarist Russia.[30] In the end *raison d'etat* will nearly always prevail, but the opposition to it is also part of history.

The difference between what was seen as the national interest and what fitted best with western ideas of self-determination has been true over recent years of the attitudes of the United States and the democracies of western Europe towards the growing evidence that the Soviet Union as a multinational empire was unravelling. Different governments made their calculations with different outcomes. On the general problems of interpretation which the challenge to Soviet rule on the Russian periphery has raised, I shall return when I come in a later chapter to what has been my major historical interest during the last part of my career as an active historian – the fall of empires.

It does, however, raise another question about the treatment of pre-revolutionary Russian history. For it would mean getting to

30.  Max Beloff, 'Lucien Wolf and the Anglo-Russian Entente, 1907–14', in *The Intellectual in Politics* (London: 1970).

grips not merely with the Russians themselves but with all the other peoples over which their empire stretched; for the USSR was territorially very close to what was the Russian Tsarist empire at the time of its greatest extent. As one of the best writers on the subject has put it, to understand the contrasting policies of the various republics that made up the USSR as Gorbachev inherited it in 1985 'a grasp of the republics' languages, histories, cultures, literatures, religions and societies is essential'.[31] Even a lifetime of study would not be enough to meet this requirement. But it stands as a warning not to imagine that solving the enigma of where Russians stand in relation to Europe is sufficient in itself.

The important elements in Russia's imperial history distinguish it from the history of the overseas empires that have collapsed during the past half-century. While the overseas empires of the European countries were mostly acquired as a result of establishing rule over peoples at a lower level of technological and social development, the western parts of the Russian empire were the fruits of military conquest over peoples who were at the same or even at a higher level of development, more clearly 'European' than the Russians themselves. In the second place, the settlement of Russians on the land in large numbers, as Curzon pointed out more than a century ago, in respect of Central Asia was a feature of Russian expansionism not only there but in European Russia and Siberia.[32] Under Soviet rule this process of settlement continued at an increasing pace. The result is the presence of a Russian diaspora throughout non-Russian parts of the Soviet Union which has made the process of imperial liquidation much harder than it was for Britain or even France with its Algerian pieds noirs. A subject that might have been thought peripheral to Russian history a generation ago has been thrust into the forefront and makes demands on the historian that could not have been foreseen.

31.  Dominic Lieven, *The Soviet Crisis* (London: Research Institute for the Study of Conflict and Terrorism, May 1991), p. 1.
32.  G. N. Curzon (later, the Marquess Curzon of Kedleston), *Russia in Central Asia* (London, 1889).

# VI

## The Jewish Experience

Some forty years ago, as I was beginning my long run as a regular reviewer for the *Daily Telegraph*, I remember being offered a book to review by H. D. Ziman, then the review editor, and saying that I would prefer not to tackle it since it dealt with Jewish history and, although a Jew, I did not have special competence in that field. Ziman consoled me by saying that in that I was not unique, and no doubt sent me off with some tome more suited to my alleged expertise. Once again, in retrospect, I had missed an opportunity. The ambience in which I grew up was, as already noted, almost wholly Jewish; in the family home the Jewish topics and controversies of the day were part of the staple of conversation. I took too little in. I had perforce learned some Hebrew for religious purposes and was reasonably familiar with the public practices of Judaism. With Hebrew and German, I should have been able to acquire Yiddish but did not.

It was not that I was unaware of the grave events affecting Jews that were taking place in Europe – the pressure for escape from discrimination in eastern Europe and later from even graver perils in Germany. I followed the efforts to get the British government to take a more positive role towards the possibilities of Palestine as a place of refuge, and, after the realities of the Holocaust sank in, was appalled by Ernest Bevin's callous indifference in the face of Jewish misery and by the methods of terrorism adopted by some Jews in their fight with the mandatory power in the last phase of Britain's ultimately ill-starred connection with the Holy Land.

What was lacking in me was not any sense of the immediacy of Jewish problems nor of their relevance even to someone by now part of the British scholarly establishment but a general historical framework in which to place the experiences of family and friends in the diaspora or Israel. My contributions to a more than ephemeral consideration of Jewish issues were thus few and the result of the occasional invitation to lecture or contribute to some collection of short pieces. I was a member for reasons of piety of the Jewish Historical Society of England but declined, again on grounds of incompetence, an offer to stand for its presidency. Perhaps because I was the first member of my family to be born in Britain, I could never get truly enthusiastic about the minute investigations into the doings of individual Jews or small Jewish communities in England, either before the expulsion or after their 'readmission'. These seemed to me matters of antiquarian rather than historical interest.

What awakened greater concern on my part was the need to provide a proper historical record for the last tragic years of the experince of European Jewry, and I set out the importance of this task in my preface to the collection of essays *On the Track of Tyranny* which I edited for the Wiener Library in 1960.[1] But I note that my own first volume of collected essays published in the same year contains nothing on a specifically Jewish theme. The same was not true a decade later, by which time I had become more closely involved with Israel, particularly in the academic field.[2]

One of these I have already referred to: 'Lucien Wolf and the Anglo-Russian Entente, 1907–1914'. I placed it in the section of the collection dealing with foreign afffairs since I did not go into detail on the Jewish background of Wolf's anti-Russian campaign. But three essays are grouped together under the heading 'The Jewish Predicament'. All are quite short and all deal with the new twist given to the age-old problem of the relations between Jews and their host societies in the diaspora by the emergence of a Jewish nation-state. It was, moreover, a nation-state that brought with it its own local problems, and its own solutions for them, which might not fit in with what Jews elsewhere saw as in the Jewish people's long-term interests, at a time when the nation-state as the prime focus of political action was itself under challenge. Two further pieces explored a particular impact that the unsolved problem of Israel's relations with its neighbours was

---

1.  Max Beloff (ed.), *On the Track of Tyranny: Essays Presented to Leonard G. Montefiore* (London: 1960).
2.  Max Beloff, *The Intellectual in Politics and Other Essays* (London: 1970).

having upon the Jewish position elsewhere, especially in France and in Britain itself. We were already witnessing that shift in sympathy of a large section of the British left from pro-Zionist to a pro-Arab position which has had many unfortunate consequences.[3]

Since I wrote these brief pieces some quarter of a century ago, my own appetite for Jewish history has been much enhanced, as have the possibilities of satisfying it. One result of the foundation of the State of Israel and of the flourishing of a large academic community within it has been a major impetus to historical research. In the early years the desire to emphasize continuity with the biblical period and the Herodian kingdom meant a con-centration upon these periods and their archaeological remains as though the intervening nineteen centuries had somehow vanished from consciousness. But as interest has shifted to the antecedents of the State itself and so to the history of the Zionist movement, the original bias has been largely overcome. Fortunately, although much work is first published in Hebrew, some of it does find its way into translation, and some Israeli scholars with a British or American background write and first publish in English.

The Zionist movement itself cannot be understood without an appreciation of the circumstances which brought it forth, so that it is in one way into the history of the diaspora itself. And studies of the diaspora in its full geographical extent in the Moslem world, as well as in Europe and North America, have likewise received much greater attention than ever before, both in Israel itself and in some centres of Jewish learning in western Europe, notably in Britain, and in the United States. Having declined to review works on Jewish history forty years ago, I now find that from 1989 to 1991 most of my reviewing was of books of direct Jewish interest for the *Jewish Journal of Sociology*.

In this new outpouring of Jewish historical writing the most obvious feature is that it departs from the somewhat inward-looking approach of earlier generations. In Israel's case it means an acceptance of its two links with the external world – the economic and cultural ties that bind it to the diaspora, and its inescapable geographical location in a part of the world where Islam and the various brands of Arab nationalism are the dominant political factors. That this local environment has been

3. 'Zionism as Nationalism', *Jewish Chronicle*, 27 August 1965; 'The Israel Haters' *Jewish Chronicle*, 21 November 1968; 'Rootless Cosmopolitans', *Encounter*, November 1969.

overwhelmingly hostile does not mean that it can be ignored. If it were to be, the Crusader castles would be there as reminders. In relation to the diaspora, vestiges of what I have called mere antiquarianism are disappearing. It is appreciated both that the character of Jewish communities has always been in part determined by their gentile surroundings, and that part of the Jewish story has been the Jews' own contribution to general history, not only in the post-emancipation period. Professor Jonathan Israel's studies of the Jewish element in European and world commerce in the seventeenth and eighteenth centuries are a case in point.[4] For the post-emancipation period, when Jews began in greater numbers to play a part in more general cultural activities – in science, literature, music and the fine arts – much work has gone into trying to assess whether their contribution has any specific characteristics deriving from an ancestral world quite distinct from that of their gentile peers.

Nevertheless there remains a central and perhaps unanswerable question. What is the subject matter of Jewish history? The whole of modern historical scholarship is based upon an often unexamined major premise, namely that history's proper subject matter is complete societies, that is to say human groupings which have in common participation in economic and social activities, specific forms of religious expression and organization, and above all their own political institutions. It need not necessarily be history of what we now call nation-states, though much of it is; we know how to deal with Greek city-states at one extreme and with empires at the other, but in every case there is some sense of the influence of a particular territory. The history of England is not just the history of what Englishmen have done, it is also the history of what has happened in England, and the landscape is part of our understanding of it. In that sense the history of the early Jewish kingdoms or of modern Israel fit perfectly well into our normal way of looking at things. But, since ancient times, the majority of Jews have not lived within the boundaries of the Holy Land – nor do they live there now. How do we define their history?

No doubt some people would say that there is an answer, that what we are dealing with is the history of a particular religious

4.   See in particular Jonathan I. Israel, *European Jewry in the Age of Mercantilism, 1550–1750* (Oxford: 1985).

community, so that Jewish history can be seen as part of the history of religion, which is a familiar field of study. And no doubt there can be a history of Judaism as there is of Buddhism or Lutheranism or any other creed. And some Jews have wished to see it as just that. If one saw oneself as some German Jews did before the catastrophe as 'Germans of the Jewish persuasion' – and they had their counterparts in other European countries – then only the religious aspect of one's past has special significance. For the rest, the history in which Jews felt themselves to be incorporated was that of Germany, England, France and the United States or any other place of abode.

In circumstances where religious allegiance was at the basis of social organization – medieval Europe or under the caliphates – such an attitude could correspond to reality at least in large measure. But it was never wholly convincing and with the coming of emancipation and the collapse of the ghetto it became untenable, since even if the Jews themselves held to it their gentile neighbours did not. One did not have to be an overt anti-semite to take a different view. In his study of the identity crisis of the German Jewish economic elite at the time of its major contributions to Germany's growing economic might, Professor W. E. Mosse was compelled to treat of families which were seen to stand apart and which had few or no social relations with their gentile counterparts, even though they no longer practised the Jewish faith and had in many instances accepted conversion to Christianity.[5]

Modern political anti-semitism, which reached its apogee in the Nazi movement, turned this perception of a common element in the Jewish communities into a fully fledged racial argument: Jews are Jews because of a common physical ancestry. Yet, quite apart from the dubious equation between race and culture, we know enough about the Jewish past to know that the idea of their common ancestry in a particular Semitic tribe is flawed. However strong the practice of endogamy may have been during some periods, it was never universal. And although Judaism has not in modern times been a missionary religion, some accretions to the Jewish physical stock must have been the result of conversions.

5. W. E. Mosse, The German-Jewish Economic Elite, 1820–1935: A Socio-Cultural Profile (Oxford: 1989); W. E. Mosse (ed.) Second Chance: Two Centuries of German-speaking Jews in the United Kingdom (Tübiajen: 1991).

Looking round the streets of Tel Aviv one would hardly identify an invariable Jewish type.

Some Jewish scholars in the contemporary world have accepted something of this racial approach in the efforts to escape from a purely religious definition of the Jewish essence. So one may be asked to accept the Jews as an 'ethnic' group, and, for instance, the Jews of the United Kingdom as an 'ethnic' minority, like the minorities of Asian or Afro-Caribbean origin, and with identical problems.[6] I find this unconvincing, because if one looks at what particular elements of individuality the Jewish community in Britain or indeed in other western democracies has been concerned to preserve, it is primarily the capacity to fulfil its religious obligations. Where this requirement impinges upon a major question like schooling, there may be a meeting point with the demands of some other groups, but this does not make the issue one of 'ethnicity'.

At the other extreme we have the view that, given the breakdown of the ghetto and the absorptive capacity of western societies as exemplified in the United States, Jewish history as such may be coming to an end and what will be left will be Israel and Israeli history alone.[7] Speculation about the future is not however the proper province of the historian, and the fact that such views have been expressed by a major historian of Zionism may give them weight but does not wholly answer the question of how Jewish history should be defined and explored.[8]

One needs to find some framework within which Jewish history can be grasped as a single story, despite its extraordinary ramifications and even though for centuries the two main branches, Ashkenazi and Sephardi (including those 'oriental' Jews who had not undergone the Spanish experience), had very little direct contact and followed different lines of development.[9] Religion would itself be insufficient to provide such a framework. But two other elements come into the reckoning.

The first is once again territorial. The connection of the Jews with their original homeland was never forgotten, and it is indeed

6. See the introduction by David Cesarini to the collected volume of which he was editor, *The Making of Modern Anglo-Jewry* (Oxford: 1990).
7. See David Vital, *The Future of the Jews* (Cambridge, Mass.:1990).
8. David Vital, *The Origins of Zionism* (Oxford: 1975); *Zionism: The Formative Years* (Oxford: 1982); *Zionism: The Crucial Phase* (Oxford: 1982).
9. The story of the Sephardi and oriental Jews is graphically set forth in Chaim Raphael, *The Road from Babylon* (London: 1985).

implicit and often explicit in their religious observances. The belief that a messiah would one day arise and return the Jews to their home was embedded in their psyche. The appearance in times of trial of 'false messiahs' would not have been comprehensible but for the messianic tradition.[10] And at the other end of the story we have the Land fulfilling its role as the focus of Zionist endeavour, and a massive in-gathering taking place.

The other element of continuity is that of language. While it is correct that Hebrew was not normally used in the diaspora for secular purposes, the need to master the language in order to partake in religious services and to study the repositories of Jewish thought ensured its survival. The fact that those who prayed in Hebrew in the synagogue spoke Yiddish or Ladino or some local language outside cannot detract from the role of the original sacred tongue.

When we come to the renewed settlement of Jews in the Holy Land over the past century or so and to the history of the embryonic Jewish state and then of the State of Israel itself, two decisions of far-reaching importance stand out. The first decision was that only the historic homeland would do – Zion could not be created except in Zion. The second was that Hebrew would have to serve for all secular purposes, and would need to be remodelled with that in mind. A corollary was that all teaching should be in Hebrew. Neither decision was taken without opposition. And both involved sacrifices. Jewish settlement did not go unopposed and Israel was fated to inherit the hostility of its neighbouring states as protagonists of local Arab claims. Learning a new language was a major hurdle for the immigrant to overcome, and could put a heavy strain on a country's intellectual resources at times of heavy influx. Foreign observers have seen the Kibbutz as the most striking Israeli institution; the Ulpan – the intensive language school – is perhaps of equal importance.

Both these aspects of the Jewish identity have played easily definable roles in the relatively brief life of the Jewish state. The threat to the Land has meant an accent on military preparedness to an extent not foreseen by most of Zionism's Founding Fathers. The army, embodying almost the entire population (of both sexes) in either an active or a reserve capacity, has been an instrument of nation-building which has only remote parallels among

---

10.   The importance of this strain in Jewish experience is well set out in Lionel Kochan, *Idols and Messiahs: The Challenge from History* (Oxford: 1990).

European nations. Language has helped obliterate the distinctions of provenance among the population and bring together the principal streams of the Jewish experience. Since with minor exceptions, oriental Jewry barely survives in its original setting, since it is a minority – perhaps one-fifth – of the world Jewish population as a whole, and since the basic institutions of the State were created by Ashkenazis and their immediate descendants, these developments could be regarded as the incorporation of the Sephardis into the mainstream. Until a short while ago, that judgement would be countered by pointing out that in Israel itself there was no such numerical Ashkenazi preponderance. But the sudden opening of the barriers to emigration from the Soviet Union looks like weighting the scales once more on the Ashkenazi side.

An attempt to estimate the consequences of a massive immigration from the Soviet Union, which most people would until quite recently have regarded as unthinkable, raises again the unsolved question of Israel's relationship to the Jewish religious inheritance which I have claimed to be the most important element in Jewish history. For, while decisions about land and language were taken and taken early, the basic decision about religion has never been taken and the question cannot indeed easily be resolved.

By the time the Zionist movement gathered momentum around the turn of the century, many European Jews had to some extent abandoned religious belief and practices and sought to be fully acculturated to their existing surroundings. They might identify with the gentile establishment as in western Europe or, in the countries where they suffered severe discrimination and even persecution, with one or other opposition or revolutionary movement. The early pioneers of the resettlement were drawn from both religious and non-religious groups. The reaction to Zionism of those who gave priority to the religious heritage was two-fold. There were those who, arguing that the return to the Holy Land was impossible until the Messiah appeared, were fundamentally opposed to the Zionist movement, retaining their opposition to the idea of a Jewish state even after their settlement in what is now Israel. Another element accepted the validity of the means but insisted on a definition of the end which was to be a Jewish state in the sense that it should be a state in which (where Jews were concerned) the precepts of religious law should prevail. For the majority of the Israeli population, however, religion has been seen (as in western liberal democracies) as a matter of personal choice, unsuitable for legal enforcement.

The problem was not and is not an insignificant one since, like the Islamic *shariah*, Jewish religious law having been developed to cover the entire life of a community impinges on many areas which are elsewhere covered by secular legislation: family law and the place of women; sabbath-keeping; dietary regulation; the recognition of membership of the national community itself in respect of particular individuals – all these are far from marginal issues. The most obvious sign of the importance of the religious question is the fact that it explains why Israel, almost alone among recently created states, has no written constitution. Since there could be no agreement when independence was proclaimed about the religious content of a constitution, it had to be forgone. The way in which Isreal's political system has developed, particularly its proportional representation system, has ensured that, while religious parties cannot expect a majority, their support is usually essential for the formation of coalition governments, so that they can insist on a fairly high level of compliance with their demands. In most of the contested areas the religious parties have hitherto prevailed.

To some extent the degree of support for the religious approach to the state and its problems has been affected by the varied provenance of successive waves of immigration. It remains to be seen what the effect will be if the very high level of recent immigration from the Soviet Union continues. For whereas previous incomers from among Ashkenazi Jews were usually not more than one generation removed from traditional Jewish observances, and in the case of most of the Sephardis came from societies where religion remained for everyone the basic criterion of identity, most of those coming from the Soviet Union have been motivated by a desire to escape the communist system and its hardships, rather than by a positive longing for or even knowledge of the ancestral homeland. Such immigrants are usually very remote from what even to secular Israelis may still be instinctive.

A quite different problem was presented from the beginning to all Jews in countries touched by the Zionist movement, that of the impact of its ultimate success upon the position of those Jews who did not themselves propose to join the exodus. While from one wing in Jewry there was, as we have seen, opposition to Zionism on religious grounds, from another wing, that of the most assimilated, there was opposition on the ground that, while a country of their own might 'normalize' the lives of Jews who actually went there, for the remainder it would introduce a new element of abnormality, the possibility of cherishing or being thought to cherish a dual allegiance. Where the basic decisions were concerned, this aspect is best illustrated by the opposition of prominent members of the Anglo-Jewish establishment, represented in Lloyd George's Cabinet by Edwin Montagu, to the issuing of the Balfour Declaration, which was the basis for the United Kingdom's subsequent acquisition of the Palestine mandate.[11] But similar objections were voiced by Jewish spokemen in Germany, France and the United States.

Historians of these events have tended to be unkind to those who took this negative view and in so far as they have been critical of the carrying out of the Zionist intentions have been more interested in the impact upon the non-Jewish inhabitants of Palestine than in the impact upon Jews remaining in the diaspora. Yet the problem envisaged by Montagu and his fellows was not an unreal one. Where anti-semitism was rampant and persecution endemic, the creation of a National Home and the State of Israel was only beneficial. They could and did provide the major asylum for those fleeing persecution, when elsewhefe doors were more or less firmly shut. The question of dual allegiance interested neither Hitler nor Stalin. When, in the Soviet case, 'Zionist' was used as a term of abuse like 'rootless cosmopolitan', it was no more specific than words like Bolshevik or Fascist have become. But, in countries where anti-Semitism was only latent, there were problems for Jews who claimed full rights in the affairs of the country in which they lived while taking part, if only at a distance, in the creation of the National Home.

After the creation of the State of Israel the problem took on a particularly acuts form in the English-speaking countries and affected Jews who were not part of the organized Zionist movement and did not wish to leave the countries where they lived but were supporters of the State of Israel and vocal in its defence. It now became evident that the early discussions of the problem of dual allegiance had been misleading because of the abstract way in which they were formulated. For most of the time and in most countries, the problem of divided loyalties does not a rise. What brings it up is when the particular host country has interests that differ or appear to differ from those of the State of Israel. And

11.   I dealt with this episode in vol. 1 of *Imperial Sunset* (London: 1969; New York: 1970. 2nd edn, London: 1987; New York: 1988). A good deal more material has now become available thanks largely to Israeli scholars, but the general picture has not been seriously affected.

this was likely to be the case when Israel became an important political and military factor in the politics of the Middle East, in which the United States. Great Britain and France all had major concerns of their own, as did in a different way the Soviet Union. The Suez affair and its repercussions are illuminating in this respect. And the launching by the government of the United States of a new 'peace process' after the Gulf War in 1991 brought the issue again to the forefront of the diaspora's concarns.

The extent to which the Jewish citizens of countries with a role in the Middle East will press their point of view depends upon a variety of circumstances. The 'Jewish lobby' in the United States has obviously had much more freedom of action and more influence than the Jewish clement in the Soviest Union has been able to command. In every case one would need to trace the policies of the countries involved towards Israel and the Arab world, and these have known their own fluctuations.

The situation of Jews is not altogether unique. Wherever one has a migration on any scale, there are bound to be, at least for a certain time, ties between those who have settled overseas and their countries of origin. The Irish in the United States and Australia come to mind. How long such ties will manifest themselves politically will vary for many reasons. Even the United States has found the 'melting pot' a less telling image than was once believed. Woodrow Wilson may have been exceptionally outspoken in referring to 'hyphenated Americans' but the phenomenon still exists and may indeed be accentuated by the unwillingness or inability of some new elements in the immigration to accept the ideal of assimilation into the American mainstream as readily as did their predecessors.

In Britain and France, while a Jewish dilemma still persists in view of the largely pro-Arab leanings of their governments, a new complication has arisen with the arrival of a large-scale Islamic migration and the apparent readiness of some of its elements to accept not herely influence but even instructions from abrcad, as was seen in Britain during the Gulf War and over the Salman Rushdie affair. But there is a difference in that Islamic centres of power and influence are diffused between a number of separate states while there is only one Israel, and on the whole diaspora Jewry has been more willing in most respects to accept the norms of the host countries than many Moslem immigrants.

It is clear that the fulfilment of Zionist aspirations and the creation of the State of Israel has effected a break with almost two millennia of Jewish history. And this in turn may tempt the historian to disregard all those elements in Jewish history which do not seem to lead to this achievement. But as with the 'Whig' view of English history, there are weaknesses in this purely teleological approach. No earlier generation of Jews could place a date on the fulfilment of the promise of return, and each had to live for itself in whatever circumstances the host countries might dictate. Until emancipation in the nineteenth century, even a common Jewish authority or representative body was non-existent. Only within individual communities could elements of leadership develop, and only then within the parameters dictated by the secular authority. Nor could the contemporary existence of the Jewish people be viewed as a whole from any single point – western and oriental Jews lived separate and different lives.

We have thus to define an approach which allows for the fact that for most of their post-exilic history Jews were deprived of much of what makes up the substance of the history of most other peoples. It was always a question of survival in the face of different levels of hostility and suspicion. All first-time visitors to Israel are taken to see the memorial to the victims of the Nazi Holocaust, and probably few have escaped without a stirring of their emotions. The political attitudes of Israelis cannot be understood without understanding the lesson that they drew from the supreme modern example of inhumanity. That lesson is that no people can rely on others to safeguard its existence or defend its rights. Jews may be victims again but must never be defenceless victims. It is an uncomfortable stance but understandable. In the light of this interpretation of recent Jewish history, the fact that the State has been able to combine priority for military defence with a democratic government is a feat too little appreciated.

The other indispensable museum is the Museum of the Diaspora in Tel Aviv. Its lesson is almost as bleak as that of the Holocaust memorial. For what it shows through documents, artefacts and tableaux is the ability that Jews have shown in the past to create for themselves not only tolerable patterns of living but even at times a considerable degree of material prosperity and the high culture that goes with it. But in every case, whether in Spain or in central Europe or in the east, whatever the degree of accultura-tion, the good times have given way before a new bout of expul-sions or persecutions, leaving only artefacts and memories behind. Similar reflections are induced by the Jewish Museum in Prague, where the exhibits consist of treasures amassed by the Nazis from historic synagogues of Czechoslovakia.

Why this dashing of hopes of peaceful coexistence should have happened so regularly must preoccupy anyone who tries to look at Jewish history as a whole. Indeed at times it might almost seem that the study of Jewish history depends very largely on an assessment of the history of anti-semitism, whether in its Christian (or Islamic) roots or in its later racial and political manifestations. Because of the Nazi experience the former may be played down at least where Christianity is concerned, despite the clear overlap in the nineteenth century between religious and political anti-semitism, notably in the Orthodox Churches. Nor can it be regarded as absent from the persistent refusal of the Vatican to recognize the State of Israel despite efforts of the Israeli government to protect the Christian Holy Places and the worshippers at them – a record which contrasts so forcibly with the desecration of Jewish Jerusalem during the Jordanian occupation from 1948 to 1967.

Modern political anti-semitism has had an even more profound effect in shaping the Jewish self-consciousness both in the diaspora and latterly in Israel itself. To be a nation of scapegoats, always at hand to blame when things go wrong, is not an easy legacy.[12] It is perhaps not surprising that some Jews have, like Karl Marx, accepted the version of their role put out by their enemies and that Jewish self-hatred has fuelled some of the manifestations of redical chic in the United States.

Yet there is also the record of the creative interaction of Jewish and non-Jewish thought, without which the Jewish national movement of the past century would not have been conceivable.[13] In this respect those historians with the most useful things to say about Jewish history have been those most familiar with the languages and literatures of the host societies in the diaspora. Jewish history is not only very hard to define; it is very hard to write.

12. A useful introduction to this subject is Robert Wistrich, *Between Redemption and Perdition: Modern Anti-Semitism and Jewish Identity* (London: 1990). See also the writings on France of Michael A. Marrus, in particular, *The Politics of Assimilation: A Study of the French Jewish Community at the Time of the Dreyfus Affair* (Oxford: 1971).
13. What can be done along these lines is magisterially illustrated in the book by Jonathan Frankel, *Prophecy and Politics: Socialism, Nationalism and the Russian Jews, 1862–1917* (Cambridge: 1981).

# VII

## *Europe: Myth and Reality*

In an account of my own engagement with historical problems and my own contributions to historical study, I see clearly the void that is created by the absence on my part of any serious study of the history of the main national groups that make up, in their interplay of rivalry and competition, the history of modern Europe. With the exception of some brief incursions into French history, which I could wish had been sustained, and of some peripheral consideration of Russia, my European bibliography is blank. For someone who has not seriously studied the history of Germany, Italy, Spain or the Low Countries, Europe must be something of an abstraction. As an undergraduate my study of Europe was confined to the High Middle Ages, where I had the good fortune to be the pupil of two teachers both renowned for their authority in their special fields of interest. So thanks to Austin Lane Poole and Evelyn Jamieson, the Ottoman Empire and the Norman presence in Sicily were more familiar to me than Bismarck, Garibaldi or Cavour.[1]

I do not think this altogether a loss. Indeed, when we are asked to study history that is 'relevant', my instinctive reply is, how do

---

1. My brief study, *The Age of Absolutism* (London: 1945) was written at the request of Sir Maurice Powicke, the editor of the series in which it appeared. Powicke is another Oxford historian to whom I owe much. The book represented a transition from my concentration on the Stuart period in England and my later concern with more recent times. It makes the nineteenth-century lacuna in my work even more visible. Thanks to generations of sixth-formers, the book remained for a long time my most lucrative piece of writing.

we know what is relevant? It is necessary to know not merely what part the Middle Ages and the Renaissance played in the conscious elaboration of history by the nationalist historians of the nineteenth century but also what actually happened and what it felt like to be alive at the time.

As I have said in the Introduction, my first impulse to look again at European history was in connection with the movement for 'European unity' after the Second World War. Two distinct questions seem to have got mixed up. Would Europe or such part of Europe as was outside the clutches of the Soviet Union benefit from the creation of common institutions for common purposes in economic, scientific and defence matters in order to promote the welfare of its citizens and prevent absorption into a Soviet or American system? And, second, was such a development in accord with an underlying sentiment of community between the nations of Europe which did not extend beyond them?

Even if these arguments were both accepted, they did not solve the question of what were to be the boundaries of such a European system. How far east could it be pushed? The question was not an actual one in the late 1940s and 1950s when the new institutions were created, since the Soviet Union would have no part in such affairs and was in a position to prevent much of central and eastern Europe from taking part either. But it presented a theoretical dilemma which has much more recently become a practical one. Various solutions have been offered, of which the least tenable was General de Gaulle's 'from the Atlantic to the Urals'. Only an ignorance of physical and human geography could make one take the view that Russia could be regarded as coming to an end at the Urals. To include only Russia west of the Urals in some European political system would be like talking of an Atlantic system today to include only the United States east of the Appalachians.

The other such question and one that has been continuously at issue has been the inclusion or non-inclusion of Britain. Britain did take part in the first creation of the European movement: the Council of Europe.[2] Since membership did not involve a sacrifice

2.  I must confess to some predilection for the Council of Europe arising from my own brief participation in its work in connection with my book, *Europe and the Europeans*, which, as I have already indicated, was an attempt to bring into some usable form discussions that had taken place under its auspices about the future course of European affairs. My enthusiasm has since

of national sovereignty over major issues of policy – it has been shown to have some domestic impact on human rights questions – it was relatively easy for Britain to figure among the founding members. And, since an adherence to democratic forms of government was made a condition of membership, other awkward questions did not arise. With later products of the movement, the European Communities, Britain has had a more uneven relationship – first excluding itself, then blackballed, then admitted, but soon to be in some respects an awkward member, showing greater reticence than most of its partners to some of the demands made upon it, both on the part of successive governments and, more importantly, on the part of the electorate.

I have recently had occasion to look again at the issue as it presented itself in the early post-war decade as exemplified by Winston Churchill.[3] Churchill is sometimes held up as one of the main advocates of a United Europe by virtue of a number of speeches made while in opposition between 1945 and 1951. But a re-examination of these texts must dispel such a belief. Participation in the Council of Europe was clearly the limit beyond which Churchill was not prepared to see Britain go.

What concerned Churchill, surveying a war-wrecked continent, was the need to avoid wars between major European powers, and with the last century and a half in mind that meant reconciliation between France and Germany, something which he had advocated after the First World War. To what extent this required supranational institutions was a matter which he was prepared to leave to the two countries themselves and to such of their continental neighbours as might feel themselves most directly affected. Since his vision was of Britain at the intersection of three political combinations, the Empire–Commonwealth, Europe and the Anglo-American partnership which he had worked so hard to bring about, it could not fit into any association that deprived it of sovereignty. To do this would destroy the Commonwealth bond and obliterate the 'special relationship' with the United States, which the emergence of the Soviet threat had

---

been tempered by my worry about the extent to which the human rights aspect has proved capable of achieving sensible marriage between two very different legal traditions – the common law and the Roman.

3. Max Beloff, 'Churchill and Europe', in W. R. Louis and Lord Blake (eds), *Churchill* (Oxford: 1992).

made more than ever essential. One is of course always entitled to argue that some historical figure would have taken a different view of some problem had he been alive today, but it is not the kind of speculation in which a professional historian should care to indulge.[4]

Churchill was well aware after his wartime experience that in matters of defence the countries of the Commonwealth would increasingly define their own interests. If necessary this might lead Britain to give undertakings to act alone. Hence the North Atlantic Treaty, binding Britain and Canada but not the rest of Commonwealth, was acceptable to those of a Churchillian out-look. Retaining a role for the US and Canada was an object to which Britain was overwhelmingly attached.[5] Some would have wished to build more upon it than a mere military alliance such as NATO became. But in retrospect such ideas were also a flight from reality.[6]

My own interest as an historian was therefore to understand the ways in which Europe's internal divisions were a real impediment to the creation of common institutions replacing the nation-states into which the impact of the French Revolution appeared to have divided it. Why did I feel, why do I feel, that the example of the United States as a working federal system is wholly inapplicable to the European scene? When working with European scholars and public figures in my Council of Europe days and later on, I came to realize how different were both the experiences and the mental constructs of the British and continental Europeans. In particular the word 'federalism' which had a precise meaning in an Anglo-

4.  The argument I have heard advanced that Churchill would have been prepared to swallow Britain's incorporation into a European Community because he espoused the plan for Anglo-French Union in 1940 seems especially weak. As I discovered in my own detailed research into that episode, which I have alluded to in my chapter on France in this volume, Churchill in June 1940 was prepared to take any step, however desperate, to keep France in the war and the French Fleet and Empire out of German hands.
5.  I stressed the North Atlantic emphasis of British policy in my book, *The Future of British Foreign Policy* (London: 1969).
6.  People tend to forget that in its early days it was expected that NATO would come to have a wider role, even extending to the cultural sphere. Of these aspirations, particularly dear to Paul-Henri Spaak as Secretary-General, the only vestige was a committee for awarding study fellowships. Of that committee I was for many years the British member.

Saxon context, meant something quite different to continental Europeans. It is not a difference that has gone away.[7]

My main concern in such writing as I engaged in was with the Americans. How could one persuade them that the United States of Europe was not something that with a little goodwill and a capacity for draftsmanship could solve all Europe's problems and even produce a new political entity which would fully subscribe to America's wider world vision?[8] I never thought this problem could be quickly solved; I do not think it has been yet. The general question of the European future and the shape of a new Europe took on a new urgency with the relaxation of the Soviet hold in eastern Europe and with Soviet talk about a 'common European home'. Was the European Community, by now including Britain, capable of indefinite expansion?[9]

It is fashionable in pro-European circles to talk about a common European culture. And of course there is a sense in which this is a fact and can be perceived on a day-to-day basis, in Britain as well as in continental Europe. One could point to the relatively painless integration of migrants from Europe into Britain or France compared to the difficulties presented by the post-colonial flow from further afield. No doubt racial and colour prejudice play a part, since these are human failings all over the world. But it is rather that the doctrine of assimilation which has been the key to dealing with past migrations cannot be easily applied to self-conscious adherents of other cultures than the European, cultures in some cases with a long pedigree.

It is one thing to accept the existence of a European culture and another to define it. Each student of the matter will approach it

7.  To this must be added the fact that in the early days the running was made largely by individuals and groups from parts of Europe where the Carolingian tradition with its Catholic overtones was important. To that tradition Britain was alien. See my essay, 'Europe from Lorraine', written in 1952 and republished in Max Beloff, *The Great Powers* (London: 1959).

8.  See Max Beloff, *The United States and the Unity of Europe* (Washington, DC: 1963). Federalism was much in vogue for areas other than Europe as well in the post-war decade. See the lecture I gave at the University of Leeds in 1953, 'The "Federal Solution" in Its Application to Europe, Asia and Africa', reprinted in Max Beloff, *The Great Powers*.

9.  For my attempt to enlighten Americans about the difficulty of such an extension see Max Beloff, 'Fault Lines and Steeples: The divided Loyalties of Europe', *National Interest*, 23 (Spring 1991). Some of this chapter takes up an argument I first set out there, though it is consistent with my earlier writings.

with his own preconceptions and preferences. I am personally inclined to regard the boundaries of European classical music tradition as very important. The music of Asia and Africa sounds different even to the untrained ear. To make music the test would be to include Russia as well as central and eastern Europe. But it would then be hard to exclude the United States. The same problems would arise if one were to seek to use literature or drama as one's touchstone. Furthermore appreciation of 'high culture' has always been the prerogative of the few, though modern media have helped numbers involved in its production and appreciation to grow more rapidly than in the past. The political problems that Europe faces reach down to the entirety of its societies and the solutions must have in the end a popular appeal.

What makes for the necessary degree of co-operation that can give scope to political organization on the local, provincial, national or eventually supranational plane is a sense on the part of those involved that they are part of the same family, cherishing the same basic moral values whether or not embodied in a religious creed or religious observances, and hence able within those limits to reconcile the demands of the individual with the needs of the whole, even to the ultimate test of risking life itself.[10] How such entities are formed and what is required for them to endure is a problem that historians of any era and any part of the world consistently face.

It is obviously all too easy to fall into the trap of thinking that the movement is all in one direction from family to tribe to world-citizenship. In nineteenth-century liberal thinking there was a predisposition to assume that the nation-state would prove, at any rate in Europe, the ultimate goal to which all societies would progress in pursuit of what it was assumed Britain and France and Spain had already achieved.[11] The themes of German and Italian 'unification' were thus staple fare, and it was believed that only external constraints prevented other nations, there as it were in

10.　Sir Michael Howard has done much to show how the relatively specialist topic of military history can be used to define and explore the viability of political communities. See *inter alia* the papers collected in Michael Howard, *The Lessons of History* (Oxford: 1991).

11.　On Spain, I must express a particular debt to Raymond Carr, *Spain, 1808–1939*. It features among the many books that came my way as a book reviewer – an occupation which does protect one against narrowness, if literary editors permit.

embryo, from following their example. Conflicts would be avoided not by the imposition of supranational institutions but by realizing that the quarrels that divided the nations – a frontier dispute here or there – would be solved peacefully so as not to interrupt the beneficent flow of commerce.

Nation-building and the relation of the nation-states to their neighbours and to Europe as a whole is always a subject for argument. Different interpretations of the nation's past may, as we have seen in the case of France, play a part in marking out political divisions. Italian historians are still divided over the respective roles of Cavour and Garibaldi and try to fit foreign historians of their country into one or other ideological camp. For Italy, however, the rise and fall of Mussolini and the Fascist Empire does not seem to have left the same mark as the Nazi experience in Germany, perhaps because the Fascist experience was a less profound one and less destructive.

Germany has had to face the fact of its unsuccessful challenge for world status or even domination in two major wars, and the knowledge of the unspeakable atrocities that marked the conduct of the second. It is not surprising that German historians – even outside the Marxist camp – should be so divided both on 'war-guilt' and the 'Holocaust' and on the question whether the ways in which Germany encountered and absorbed the industrial revolution help to explain why it failed there to give rise until latterly to the pacific bourgeois type of society and liberal–democratic institutions that have marked other western industrial countries. Was German experience truly different and was its form of totalitarian immersion something unique or alternatively understandable in the light of other totalitarian experiences, whether of the left or right?

Such questions go so far into the roots of the nation's self-consciousness and affect such practical problems as what young Germans should be taught about their own recent history that foreign historians must treat them with particular care. It is not a theme which I myself have ever found it possible to tackle.[12] To

12. Two recent articles have helped to illustrate the controversies among German historians on these issues: Jurgen Kocka, 'German History before Hitler: The Debate about the German Sonderweg', *Journal of Contemporary History*, XXIII (1988), and Beatrice Heuser, 'Museums, Identity and Warring Historians: Observations on History in Germany', *Historical Journal*, XXX (1990).

mention such issues is enough to emphasize that the exiles in Victorian London who plotted or followed the creation of the new nation-states in continental Europe were over-optimistic in their belief that a Europe of such states would be a more peaceable and creative one.

Even where nation-states were thought to be grounded in popular sentiment and viable institutions, flaws have revealed themselves and dissident minorities have reared their heads. Public education and literacy, once seen as major elements in nation-building, have shown themselves able to act as catalysts for fission. The Europe of the nations has proved no more stable and enduring than the seventeenth- and eighteenth-century Europe of the dynasties.[13] The imposition of external force has for periods maintained a semblance of overall control but has rarely done much to extinguish historical rivalries and even hatreds. It may even create new ones. The reunification of Germany may have given rise to more long-lasting problems than its original unification. If there is one thing that can be said of Europe 'from the Atlantic to the Urals' or, as I would prefer it, 'from Donegal to Kamchatka', it is the high degree of political and social instability that it presents.

It is necessary, in order to understand the sources of instability, to get away from the nineteenth-century idea that there is somewhere a model European system consisting of nations which can be defined precisely and accurately placed on the map. Even France, the model for students of nations, at least in its own eyes, is, as I have shown in an earlier chapter, as much a deliberate creation of statecraft as any other. Corsicans continue to make the point. We do not need the Basques and Catalans to emphasize that Spain even after half a millennium of central rule does not present the picture of a single nation at ease with itself. Irish, Scottish and Welsh problems continue to figure in the politics of what we still refer to as the United Kingdom.

One has to look at the whole picture from quite a different point of view, taking European history from the Dark Ages as a single subject of study in which no period is irrelevant. What does one find then?

In the first place the view propagated by nationalist his-

---

13. My book, *The Age of Absolutism*, deals with the transition from monarchical to popular despotism.

toriography and literary sentiment that Europeans have normally lived and died on the same spot and have a life experience limited geographically and disturbed only by the thrust towards the cities that came with the industrial revolution is a fiction. During most of Europe's history, the continent has been the scene of continual migration, sometimes from east to west, sometimes in the contrary direction, as with the Germans from the early Middle Ages and into the eighteenth century. The extent to which indigenous peoples have been displaced or assimilated into the people of the conquerors is a question difficult to answer, particularly for the periods for which only archaeological evidence is available. Not all migration is the fruit of conquest.

As with the current movement from east to west and now indeed across the Mediterranean from south to north, it may be simply the attraction of real or presumed economic opportunities. What can be said is that there have always been movements of population and that these have left their mark.

One does not need to enter into the vexed field of racial identification to deal with the major legacy of these movements, which is the more concrete one of language. Language is by far the most important element in political self-identification and the issue which more than any other has dominated European politics and now bids fair, along with religion, to dominate the Indian sub-continent. The spread of literacy, the abandonment in Europe of Latin as the lingua franca for administrative purposes, as with English in India, and the growth in the domestic functions of the state – all these have made it more and more important to people to see how far their native tongue is able to carry them in their search for economic and social upward mobility. To some extent linguistic assimilation has proved possible in major states and in some lesser ones, but it has never been complete.

Language thus forms the basis for any realistic map of political Europe, but to the complexity of the linguistic pattern religion has added another and sometimes associated source of division. If we leave out the unique case of the Jews, to which I have already referred, only two religions have seriously contested for a place in Europe – Christianity and Islam. From the first advance of the Islamic drive into the west no active religious community survives. The Moors of Spain are known by their artistic legacy only. Moslem communities along the Mediterranean littoral of western Europe are the product of recent migration, not of historical conquests.

More lasting have been the results of Turkish conquests in the south-east. The Balkans still contain sizeable Moslem communities, some of them Turkish-speaking, which add to the European mosaic. Turkish rule has also had, in the opinion of many people, a permanent influence over the political attitudes and practices of the non-Moslem peoples subjected to it over the centuries. One of the important fault lines in European politics would thus be the former outer limits of the Turkish Empire in Europe, brought to general consciousness again by the Yugoslav crisis that gathered momentum in 1991.

Most of Europe was, however, for centuries dominated by the Christian Churches, a fact whose full importance our own secular age in western Europe may find it hard to assimilate. From the political point of view, two more fault lines were created during the periods of major ecclesiastical influence. There was first the division between those parts of Europe whose Christianity came from Constantinople and those to whom it came, directly or indirectly, from Rome. The source of people's particular brand of Christianity made an important difference in many respects, including a different perspective on Church – State relations. But the most immediate and lasting significance has been in the relatively straightforward matter of the local language's written script. This difference has been particularly important among the southern Slavs. But, wherever the adherents of the two religions have clashed along Russia's western and south-western borders or in Transylvania and among the southern Slavs, it has proved especially difficult to create durable and acceptable political structures.

The second fault line is that within western Christendom created by the Protestant Reformation, which in turn built upon some elements of dissidence in earlier centuries. As between Catholic and Orthodox further east, the boundaries of the two religious allegiances were fixed by war. The issue was mainly decided by 1648, but subsequent persecutions and migrations to some extent tidied up the map. The extraordinary view held in some quarters that 'kings and battles' are matters of secondary interest not affecting the mainstream of human development could not be more wrong. What would have been the religious map of Europe had the Battle of Lepanto or the Battle of the White Mountain gone the other way?

Britain is not an exception to the general importance to be attached to the wars of religion, even if it managed to achieve in its ecclesiastical settlement under Elizabeth I a national Church that could claim to be at once Protestant and Catholic.

The history of Ireland, north and south, is a very clear case of the importance of early decisions about religious allegiance. It is difficult to see why Britons should find Ukrainian politics hard to fathom when they have Ireland on their doorstep.

Language and religion then provide the base for making sense of European history. There are of course many other divisions that have manifested themselves in attempts to build 'European' institutions. For instance, England and Ireland (like Australia, New Zealand and above all the United States) are common law countries. Scotland and western European countries are in the Roman law tradition, modernized in the latter case in the Napoleonic Codes. In early modern Russia as in Asia, law was the sovereign's will and the attempt to bring Russia within the legal world of the rest of Europe was frustrated by the Bolshevik Revolution.

The more disturbing element, however, has been commerce. When looking at the result of wars it is tempting to see mountains and rivers and sea-coasts as the conditioning factors. But this is partially misleading. Mountains do indeed form barriers to the march of armies and even to settlement; but they are not conclusive barriers, or Italy would never have been invaded and there would be no German-speakers in the Upper Adige (alias the South Tyrol). Rivers and coast-lines have for most of Europe's history been the avenues for the passage of men and goods. (Only in the eighteenth century did road-building pick up from where the Romans left off.) The North Sea and the Baltic formed for centuries a trading world of which the now defunct Germanic settlements on the Baltic coast were the visible sign. The Rhine and the Danube and their tributaries form further arteries (like the Dnieper and the Volga), without which neither Europe's demographic nor its material nor its cultural history are intelligible.[14]

14.  I owe much to the recent book *The Danube* by Claudio Magris (London: 1989). Written originally in Italian by the Professor of German Literature at the University of Trieste, the book shows how, taking a look at a much fought-over part of Europe – Trieste itself has been contested between Yugoslavs and Italians since it ceased to be the Habsburg Empire's main port – through tracing a river that winds its way through it, old and new connections can be shown to survive even where modern politics demands

Since commercial enclaves have a political and military con-
notation it is not surprising that the inhabitants of the interior
may turn against them: Spoleto becomes Split, Ragusa becomes
Dubrovnik and Danzig Gdansk. In English (though not Irish)
history, place-names were settled for good quite early on. But in
central and eastern Europe the changes of political control have
obliterated names from the map that seemed well established in
the year of my birth, 1913. It could be argued that stability of
frontiers has been more marked in western than eastern Europe.
But these frontiers have been the product of the same forces. We
were brought up to believe that the conflict between the Spanish
monarchy and the Dutch was one in which the sturdy Protestantism
of the Dutch overcame the less determined resistance of their
southern brethren. It was a thesis which appealed to the typical
nineteenth-century American Protestant liberal historian, John
Lothrop Motley. In this century the eminent Dutch historian
Pieter Geyl showed that the boundary was fixed along the line of
division between opposing armies which could go no further.
As a result the modern kingdom of the Netherlands is a country
with one language but two religions, while modern Belgium is a
country with two languages and one religion.[15]

Central and eastern Europe had the cruellest time. The
Treaties of Versailles and St Germain tried to apply national self-
determination to areas in which the mingling of populations
prevented a clear-cut answer as to where boundaries should come
and were denounced by historians and politicians for favouring the
victors. Imperial Germany in the Treaty of Brest-Litovsk in 1918
had shown that a victor can go even further and not take self-
determination for granted. Hitler was to go further still and
attempt to simplify the redrawing of the map by a tidying up
process of massacres and deportations. A further simplification was
the result of the westward flight of Germans after Hitler's defeat.
But the simplification was incomplete and proved inadequate.
What kept east Europe at peace was the imposition of Russian rule

separation. There is always profit in being reminded of a new perspective
on what may otherwise seem well-established features. I could compare the
impact with that made upon me over half a century ago by David Mathew's
book, *The Celtic Peoples and Renaissance Europe* (London: 1933).

15. In *The Oxford History of Modern Europe*, the two countries are rightly
treated together. E. H. K. Kossman, *The Low Countries, 1780–1940*
(Oxford: 1978).

after 1945, itself assisted by new forced movements of peoples. Yet, with Russia's weight removed, the old fault lines, linguistic and religious, at once reappeared. Czechoslovakia has not, like its inter-war predecessor, had to deal with unreconciled Germans. But Bohemia and Moravia, once ruled from Vienna, again find it hard to get along with Slovakia, with its enduring legacy of rule from Budapest and the clericalism that derives from the role of the Church as the repository of Slovak nationalism.

It may be that the kind of knowledge that one might acquire by looking at the past in this way is irrelevant, that what one has to do is to estimate the likely result of the growing differentiation between the new core of transnational business – Milan to Zurich, to the Ruhr to Paris to Antwerp, to Rotterdam and perhaps, if the Channel Tunnel works as expected, to London and Birmingham – and the less favoured regions of its periphery. I have never thought that historians are particularly good at interpreting current trends in human affairs, though not all of my colleagues would agree. All I have done in this chapter is to indicate where, if I had another professional life to live, I would think my studies best directed.

# VIII

## The Fall of Empires

*Il est tout a fait naturel que l'on ressent la nostalgie de ce qui était l'Empire, tout comme en peut regretter la douceur des lampes à l'huile, la splendeur de la marine à voile. . . . Mais quoi? Il n'y a pas de politique qui vaille en dehors des réalités.*

Charles de Gaulle

In the original planning of my book, *Imperial Sunset*, I had intended to write a third volume taking the story through the period of disintegration of the imperial and ultimately also of the Commonwealth system between the Second World War and the 1960s. My decision not to proceed beyond 1942 and to leave it to younger scholars to pursue the theme was no doubt due in great part to the impossibility at an advanced age of undertaking a large scheme of historical research without the advantages of an academic base. But it was probably also the result of the increasing distance I have felt from other historians working in the field, which may incidentally help to explain why so much less attention was paid by potential reviewers to the second volume as compared with the first.

*Imperial Sunset* was an account of what Professor Kennedy has taught us to call 'imperial over-stretch'.[1] It sought not to probe the reasons for striving to maintain and even expand a British world system or the moral justification for doing so but simply to account for the weaknesses and inherent contradictions which were rendering the task more difficult of achievement. The war of 1939–45, which left Britain itself much diminished and saw the rise of two powers of a differing order of magnitude, made the subsequent abandonment of empire, though not the details of retreat, probably inevitable. Here I would have no choice but to agree with a new generation of historians, both British and American, who have told the story in whole or in part. Where I

---

1. See Paul Kennedy, *The Rise and Fall of the Great Powers: Economic Change and Military Conflict from 1500 to 2000* (London: 1988).

differ from them is whether the right response is to shout 'hurrah', as they do, or to murmur 'alas', as is my own instinct. It is difficult to write history, which is to some extent always a collective enterprise, if one feels oneself isolated from one's fellow workers.

What I take to be the governing philosophy of the dominant Anglo-American school is the belief in the universal application of the Wilsonian idea of national self-determination. It is taken for granted that good government can only be the product of self-government, that periods during which Europeans or (to a lesser extent) North Americans held political sway over non-Europeans were an unfortunate interruption to the political, economic and cultural development of non-European peoples, who, once they achieved their independence, would devise systems of government and patterns of development that would enable them to make up for lost time and prove them to be at least the equal of any European nation.

It has thus become almost obligatory to profess 'anti-colonialism' and admiration and respect for the Third World. It is interesting and perhaps significant that, until the upheaval in the Soviet Union from the mid-1980s on, the ideological drive of anti-colonialism was directed almost exclusively against those empires which had been the product of maritime expansion and omitted from consideration similar claims for self-determination that might be advanced by the non-Russian nationalities of the Soviet Union.[2]

What Wilsonians overlooked was that, in dealing with Europe, President Wilson and his like were dealing with countries many of which had a high degree of national consciousness, in most cases a history of independent political existence before their incorporation into empires that the First World War had brought to an end, and with few exceptions a political class that could operate the machinery of a modern state. Their frontiers were indeed contested because of the wayward location of national minorities but they were frontiers which for the most part reflected their own past – they were not the straight lines drawn upon the map by the imperial powers which form the frontiers of post-colonial Africa. One cannot say that Wilsonian ideas proved totally successful in

2.   The European empires were the objects of hostile intervention by both the Russians and the Americans, though for differing reasons. See Max Beloff, 'Reflections on Intervention', *Journal of International Affairs*, XXII (1968), reprinted in *The Intellectual in Politics and Other Essays* (London: 1970).

the Europe of Versailles, but they did at least provide a plausible approach to some of its problems. And they are now, with the retreat of Russian power, undergoing something of a revival. But in most of the Third World the basic preconditions do not exist, and have never existed.

I would not, however, base my dissent from current orthodoxy upon abstract formulae. An outsider cannot without difficulty measure political or social success. What he can do is look at something much simpler, what used to be known as the 'condition of the people'. And this we can do more easily than in the past, with the great growth in reporting both on the printed page and through the electronic media. Indeed what I ask myself about the 'anti-colonialist' school of historians is simply, 'Do they read the newspapers?'

I begin with the presumption that, with the possible exception of some religious enthusiasts desirous of martyrdom, most human beings in all societies wish to live out in peace the span of their natural lives. For this reason, wherever the retreat of empire leads to large-scale bloodshed, one must ask whether the people in question have actually benefited from the imperial retreat. Where such conflicts also help to engender famine, as is the case in Ethiopia and the Sudan and Somalia as I write, the same query must be raised.

I also assume that people in general wish to have at least a decent level of subsistence for themselves and their families, adequate food, clean water, and the clothing and housing appropriate to the particular climate. They also expect that, in so far as their subsistence is the result of their own labours, they will not be wantonly deprived of it to swell the pockets of their rulers. It is not difficult to show that colonial regimes extracted part of the product of the peoples concerned for the benefit of overseas investors or for support of expatriate administrators. The question is whether, in the new situation, more is not being siphoned off, for fewer services, and in many cases to maintain military establishments far in excess of any serious fears about the country's defence

In so far as the anti-colonialists do admit worries about the countries whose paths to independence they have charted with such glee, they are more likely to be focused on the presence (or more commonly absence) of democratic forms of government and of 'human rights', including political rights as defined by the west. Yet what would seem more important than the existence of a multi-party system or free elections is a measure of competence on the part of the rulers, whatever their legitimacy in democratic terms. It is, with some notorious exceptions, the incompetence of the successor governments rather than their tyranny which is the more hurtful to the peoples they now rule.

Much of what goes wrong is held to be the result of the previous era of colonial rule, but as that period recedes it is possible to see that the most damaging of all imports from the west has been in the realm of ideas. It is the folly of collectivist economics and of state-planning as preached by western or western-trained ideologists that has been at the root of so-called 'African socialism' and has made it possible for the Nkrumahs, Nyereres and Kaundas to wreak havoc on the promising economies they inherited at the time of independence. Where the Soviet Union itself has intervened to uphold regimes of its own brand of socialism – Cuba, Ethiopia, Angola, Mozambique – the results have been even more catastrophic for the peoples concerned.

All major political transitions are attended with violence. No one would pretend that the European empires were not largely installed by force or would exclude from history the losses inflicted upon those subjected to them. It was colonies of settlement where the losses inflicted upon the defeated were most severe, which is why it is so ironical that Americans and Australians should rank themselves as anti-colonialists. And what was true of the creation of empires was equally true of their collapse and disappearance from the scene. One cannot condemn what is in the nature of things. For that reason it was possible in the early years of Indian independence to take a restrained view of the upheavals and massacres that accompanied the 'transfer of power'. The belief that the unity of the sub-continent, first imposed by the British Raj, would survive its demise was always far-fetched. It was possible to look benevolently on the early political development of India and Pakistan as independent nations and, in India's case particularly, to admire the degree to which impartial administration, the rule of law and democratic practices seemed to have taken root.

Gradually, however, the grounds for optimism even for the sub-continent have been stripped away. Pakistan and India have used up their resources in political rivalry and military preparations and conflicts, turning the area into a key arena for the Cold War. Pakistan itself failed to maintain its original unity and was split into two states, neither of which has shown signs of doing more than alternating between military and civilian regimes, none of them capable of reconciling the different elements of which their countries were composed. In India it begins to look as though with the passing of the last generation of those leaders formed by the Raj, even if in opposition to it, the fractures of religion and race, of caste and language, increasingly call into question the country's ability to function as a united, secular and tolerant republic. The capacities that Indians have shown for economic entrepreneurship in the parts of the world to which they migrated are vitiated at home by the heavy-handedness and corruption of an overweening administration. Now that over forty years have elapsed since the end of British rule, it is time these facts were included in any assessment of the fruits of independence.

In writing therefore about the last stages of the British Empire, one would not now be able to judge the successive proclamations of independence for this or that country or territory without regard to what came after. But, confronted as one is with new developments from day to day or year to year, the task is so difficult that no one is to be blamed for fighting shy of it. We could not now endorse what was once the accepted formula, treating it as a transition from an empire based upon subordination to the centre to a Commonwealth system of nominal equals. As I tried to show in the second volume of *Imperial Sunset: Dream of Commonwealth*, the idea had profound weaknesses even when only countries of predominantly British settlement or at any rate European settlement were included. Once the way was open for countries with no nominal allegiance to the Crown and with independent and sometimes antagonistic cultures to become full members of the Commonwealth, the difficulties inevitably multiplied. From being an organ at least of inter-governmental co-operation on major issues of world economics and politics, the Commonwealth rapidly became no more than an umbrella for covering a limited number of technical, educational and aid projects which could probably have come into being or have subsisted without it.

Such an outcome should not have been surprising, given that, on every major issue that has divided world opinion from the Korean War to the Gulf War in 1991, members of the Commonwealth have found themselves on opposed sides. What has given the Commonwealth its only political *raison d'être* for some two decades has been the determination to root out apartheid in South Africa. Yet the means chosen to attain this end – whether sporting or cultural boycotts or economic sanctions – have been foolish and ill-considered. Once again, it is the pursuit of theoretical rather than practical goals that has been the root of evil. South Africa is the only country in Africa south of the Sahara which has the productive capacity and the skills to make up for the crying and growing deficiencies of the rest of the continent. A policy untainted by political ideology would have other countries doing everything within their power to increase investment in South Africa and thus create a demand for labour which would have forced a rapid abandonment of the racial barriers to industrial and agricultural advance. Now, with the situation changing because of new perceptions by the country's rulers, it is impossible to say whether political and economic realism will triumph over the dogma of 'one man, one vote' in a unitary state, and the socialist nostrums which African nationalists have absorbed in exile and now wish to apply at a time when the countries of the former Soviet Union are trying to shake them off. It is to credit of the British government after 1979 that it tried to act as a brake upon the folly of sanctions, even though they have been supported by the United States, which in this, as in so many other issues of foreign policy, is a prey to the ignorance and electoral calculations of congressmen.

South Africa and Israel are often referred to as the two pariah states and have indeed, because of their isolation from their neighbours, been driven into various forms of association, industrial and perhaps military. But the parallel is of course not so much in their situations internationally as in their neglected potential. South Africa has the potential to take the lead in the economic resurgence of Africa; Israel could have helped through its mastery of dry-farming techniques to solve the problems of Middle Eastern and North African economies where water-shortage is a key factor. Israel has been unable to do so because of the determination of its neighbours to obliterate it from the map, and because of the boycott they have maintained pending the achievement of that aim.

Nor are these examples of the chronic incapacity of Third World countries to see where their advantages might lie the only reason for connecting in this way an African with a Middle Eastern problem. Writing on the morrow of the war in the Gulf and its aftermath of destruction and massacre, one is inclined to think that the Arab lands have suffered three times from the demise of empires. Turkish rule was harsh and uncongenial but it did preserve a degree of stability. The Allies in the First World

War divided up its legacy and produced some possibility of economic advance through the development of the area's resources,
notably oil.[3] They too disappeared after the Second World
War, and the US hegemony that in part replaced them has been
shown to lack the capacity for constructive engagement with the
problems of the region, because of its preoccupation with external
threats as it defined them and its basic unwillingness to understand the dynamics of empire. Arab society has proved even less
capable than Indian society of overcoming the divisions of religion
and tribe, despite the advantages of a common tongue, absent in
India, and the common Islamic inheritance.[4] What has succeeded
empire has been either traditionalist regimes trying to insulate
themselves from foreign cultures while enjoying the fruits of
foreign techniques, or one-party or one-man dictatorships likewise
maintaining themselves by force and with no apparatus for the
peaceful transfer of power. Even Egypt, the most hopeful component of the Arab world, is being driven by demographic and
economic pressures to walk an ever more precarious tightrope
between anarchy and fundamentalist totalitarianism.[5] There has
been much sympathetic writing about the sufferings of Beirut, but
no one asks whether it was not better off under the Turks or the
French than as the capital of 'independent' Lebanon.

To emphasize these negative aspects of the retreat from empire
is then to find oneself out of touch with most bien-pensant
academic opinion on issues as they arise. Now that only the
vestiges of the imperial system remain, such occasions have
become rarer.[6] More important they inhibit the writing of history
because of one's own involvement in the controversies. In
1990–1, the historical profession in Britain was involved in

---

3. For the dismemberment of the Ottoman Empire, see David Fromkin, *A
   Peace to End All Peace: Creating the Modern Middle East, 1914–1922*
   (London: 1989).

4. For an illuminating discussion of the difficulty of creating modern states
   where Islamic universalism prevails, see P. J. Vatikiotis, *Islam and the State*
   (2nd edn, London: 1991).

5. For the historical roots of Egypt's problems, see P. J. Vatikiotis, *The History
   of Modern Egypt* (4th edn, London: 1991).

6. The Suez crisis of 1956 is in this respect very revealing. Most of my
   academic colleagues unhesitatingly condemned the British action; I did not.
   See W. R. Louis and Roger Owen (eds), *Suez 1956: The Crisis and Its
   Consequences* (Oxford: 1989). My own contribution to this volume, 'The
   Crisis and Its Consequences for the British Conservative Party', examines
   one deeply divisive factor in British politics at the time.

an argument about the date up to which history teaching in secondary school should come and what span of years should properly be tackled as current affairs. What struck me was the apparent self-confidence of those who asserted their ability to give an unbiased account of quite recent events whose consequences were still unfolding. Since the cause of 'contemporary history' was generally, though not exclusively, espoused by the political left, one must assume that those who were confident in their ability to teach it impartially simply assumed that their version was the only possible one.

Any new approach to an historical problem is bound to have its positive as well as negative aspects. And there is no doubt much to be gained from histories that seek to illumine the individual development of particular parts of the Empire–Commonwealth, encompassing their history before, during and after their subordination to the imperial power. Indian and African history can only benefit from such treatment. The imperial period may come to be seen as an interlude only. It is noticeable indeed that the divisions threatening Indian unity are more directly relevant to the Sikh secession from the main Hindu body and to the Mughal conquest than anything emanating from the imposition of the Raj.

One's admiration for such writings is enhanced by the thought that their authors require a range of skills – linguistic, archaeological, perhaps anthropological – which were not needed by those who wrote the history of the Empire–Commonwealth from sources available in Britain and in English.

Yet the products of this scholarship – *The New Cambridge History of India*, for instance – may prove to be only the fruit of a passing phase. It seems more than likely that the histories of all the countries once part of the British Empire will come to be written almost exclusively by citizens of those countries, just as we expect our histories of Canada and Australia to be written by Canadians and Australians. The repatriation of history is already beginning. It is likely that it will involve those who participate in it in some degree of obeisance to nationalist myths, particularly where, as in much of Africa, internally generated written sources are lacking. Indeed myth-making is a necessary part of creating a national spirit – a fact familiar to those acquainted with American historical writings in the first couple of generations after independence. Nor are European exemplars lacking.

I can foresee little resistance in Britain to such myth-making, fortified as it is by the contributions of film and television. In

March 1991, I attended at Austin, Texas, an historical conference on the subject of Winston Churchill. The general consensus among the assembled historians, British, American, and
Indian, was that he was of course a very great man but that his
'imperialism' must be regarded as a defect to be castigated. To
admit that Churchill's gloomy forebodings about the future of
India and Egypt have actually been proved accurate was too much
for these scholars to accept. I felt like a flat-earther at a conclave
of astronomers.

Whether fruitful dialogue will be possible between the protagonists of the various brands of national history that are likely to
succeed imperial history, leading ultimately to some new picture,
is an open question. Much will depend on whether these histories
are written in English or in the various vernaculars. Where the
imperial preserve has been brief or informal, English will obviously
not be the natural medium. Already to follow recent history in
the Middle East, one needs (without speaking of documentary
sources) to be able to cope with Arabic and Hebrew. Furthermore what is to be the future of English itself now that it has
become the lingua franca in so much of the world? One is told by
linguists that in the spoken form important differences are already
emerging – how will this affect the way in which it is written?
Will English as my generation had it drummed into us come to be
like Latin in relation to the 'romance' languages, increasingly
limited in its use to formal purposes? I must admit, although I
have spent much of my time reading American works on history
and politics, that I find them increasingly hard to follow. It
becomes more and more like reading a foreign language that one
knows quite well, but is not one's natural mode of expression.

One's attitude towards the collapse of the overseas empires is
bound to be affected by developments in Europe that have come
to overshadow what is going on in the Third World. The reaction
among the peoples of the former Soviet Union to its failing
economy and increasing deprivation gave rise to claims for
independence or at least very far-reaching autonomy on the part
of those Soviet republics which were brought together by the
Tsars or their communist successors to form the largest land-based
empire since the fall of Rome.[7] As each constituent part of the

---

7.  For a brief but impressive survey of the Soviet scene as it stood at the end of
    1988, see Dominic Lieven, *Gorbachev and the Nationalities*, No. 216 of
    *Conflict Studies* (London: 1988).

empire discovered more and more of its own individuality, racial, religious, linguistic, cultural, including above all the central core – Russia – all the familiar elements in a post-imperial situation begin to make themselves apparent, in particular the difficulty of tampering with frontiers when at every turn there are minorities within minorities. Anti-colonialist historians, who could always side with the indigenous peoples against their European 'oppressors', find the dissolution of an empire of this kind much harder to deal with. Do you support the Georgians against the Russians or the South Ossetians against the Georgians?

The colonial experience can of course be exemplified on a scale much smaller than that of the British, Russian, Habsburg or Ottoman Empires. Events in Yugoslavia after the death of Marshal Tito followed a pattern curiously similar to that of the Soviet Union after the death of Brezhnev. The history of Yugoslavia, though its existence dates only from the settlement after the First World War, has like the Soviet Empire much deeper historical roots, to which its component parts can refer to bolster their claims. During the period between the decline of the Byzantine Empire and the establishment of the Ottoman domination in the sixteenth century, the Balkans in general, and what is now Yugoslavia in particular, saw a many-sided struggle between local potentates into which external forces constantly intervened: Venetians, Genoese, Hungarians, Normans, Angevins, the Papacy.[8]

For a brief period in the fourteenth century, the dominant power was that of the Serbian Empire.[9] Even during this period, as during its subsequent decline, Serbia's rulers did not escape challenge either from within or from outside their realm. The Serbian Empire's frontiers, its centres of gravity and ethnic composition varied with military victories and defeats and with the changing allegiances of feudal or tribal chieftains. At the

---

8. For the Byzantine aspect of the story, see D. Obolensky, *The Byzantine Commonwealth: Eastern Europe, 500–1453* (London: 1971).
9. See Thomas Durham, *Serbia: The Rise and Fall of a Medieval Empire* (York: 1989). This close-packed narrative of warfare, treaties, marriages, murders and massacres with little attempt at analysis is difficult reading. But it may be that this depiction of an apparently arbitrary sequence of events, most of them unpleasant, effectively recreates the experience of life in the Balkans in those times. For more recent developments see Christopher Cviic, *Remaking the Balkams* (London: 1991).

height of Serbia's power, Belgrade was outside the empire. Like so many other peoples in east-central Europe, Poles, Czechs, Hungarians, Serbs can summon up claims to different and dispersed territories according to the year taken as a benchmark. When the peacemakers of 1919 summoned Yugoslavia into existence, they believed they were following the principles of national self-determination; what they were in fact doing, as seen by the Serbs, was resurrecting an empire. Hence the civil war that broke out in 1991.

It is very tempting to feel that some common explanation should encompass the falls of all empires. It is a temptation to be resisted.

Looking forward even in a speculative fashion is for an historian only a reason for looking back. My reservations about the results of the triumph of anti-colonialism may prove as ill-founded after a time as the original euphoria of its protagonists. Some Russians regret Brezhnev, even Stalin. All one can try to do is not to be carried away by fashionable slogans. But one does not need to be an historian of universalist pretensions, a Spengler or Toynbee, to be aware that there has been a record of the rise and fall of empires and that their fall has been followed by 'times of troubles' and the creation of smaller units of political sovereignty and ultimately new empires. We lack the knowledge and the mental reach to decide *a priori* that people are better or worse off when living within an imperial system than when dependent upon smaller units for their well-being and survival.

The variety of ways in which men have organized themselves socially and politically is enormous, even when we confine ourselves to periods and areas with which we have some acquaintance. People have managed to live and propagate their kind and even prosper in city-states, in monarchies, absolutist or feudal, in republics, oligarchical and democratic, and in empires. One can plunge into one chosen corner of study and see what emerges. But the historical approach does not come naturally to some people. It is to some extent an artificial abstraction, some would say a distraction from the tasks at hand. Gandhi, who for Churchill was an impudent 'half-naked fakir', was, and remains for many people, a seer and a sage.

Nations cannot stand back far enough from their own struggles to see themselves in the round. Empires may be accused of discrimination between various subject peoples in accordance with religious or racial criteria. But imperial rulers are also capable of a larger view, of looking to the benefit of the system as a whole. Their main contribution to subsequent racial conflicts has often been the encouragement they have given, usually for economic reasons, to the movements of peoples. So their inheritors find themselves not with tidy and coherent nations, but with entrenched and anxious minorities. Malaysian governments since independence have accused the British of 'racialism' because of their hostility to sanctions against South Africa – yet to know members of Chinese or Indian communities in Malaysia is to know the extent of the discrimination practised against them.

I would not claim any particular privilege for my own views about the fall of empires and the British Empire in particular, only that the time has not yet arrived and may not arrive for decades or even centuries when a final assessment could reasonably be offered. It is a pity that failure to observe the current pieties should be treated as an offence against the proper canons of scholarship. In 1987, I tried in a talk at the Royal Institute of International Affairs to sketch the views I had formed as a result of fifty years' membership of that institution. They did not accord with the general atmosphere of warmth towards the Third World and Gorbachev's Soviet Union that were the orthodoxy of the time. My talk was not reproduced in the Institute's *Journal* and to get it into print I had to seek elsewhere.[10]

I would not claim that my opinions on the contemporary scene were the better founded because of my long immersion in historical studies; what I do claim is that the absence of historical perspective as well as an unwillingness to face brutal facts explain many decisions in public policy that are otherwise a mystery. What I feel at the end of my professional odyssey is that a greater depth and hence a longer perspective would have made me more satisfied with what I have myself been able to contribute to the common fund.

While I was concluding the writing of this book, I had the chance to compare some of my conclusions and attitudes with those of a more productive and more distinguished historian, a decade junior to myself, Sir Michael Howard. A new collection of his lectures and occasional papers shows him to be someone

10. Max Beloff, 'The View from St James's Square', *National Interest*, 16 (Summer 1988). It is fair to add that the then Director of Chatham House, Admiral Sir James Eberle, denied that any political censorship was involved in not printing my lecture in the Institute's journal.

deeply concerned about the role of historical studies and above all with their relevance to contemporary problems.[11] Sir Michael's area of specialization, Europe since the French Revolution, and particularly its wars and preparations for war, has been different from my own, but the kind of issues with which we have concerned ourselves have not been so far apart.

Sir Michael is much more convinced than I am that history should be at the service of laymen and that historical studies for their own sake are a form of self-indulgence. At the same time, he is less convinced than I am of the possibility of there being an objective set of facts of which the historian must regard himself as the servant. He is thus more disposed than I would be to say that history exists only in the mind of the historian – a position which may have ample philosophical justification but which also has its clear dangers. When it comes to the application of what we have learned or think we have learned from history, the difference would seem to be one of temperament rather than anything in the nature of the problems themselves. While Sir Michael is no less convinced than I am that the twentieth century, so far from justifying the idea of progress inherited by the nineteenth century from the Enlightenment, has been an age of cumulative horrors, he remains at heart optimistic about the outcome of many changes that the vast acceleration in human affairs has brought about.

Where I think that nearly all professional historians not encumbered by compulsory adherence to a specific ideology would agree is that the 'lessons of history' cannot be applied in any simple or mechanical fashion. No two series of events ever reproduce each other completely; some victories induce hubris, others do not; some revolutions have their Thermidor, others avoid it. All one can hope to have are suggestions and intimations that set the imagination working. This is a far cry from the pretensions of the social scientists, whose belief in strict causality has over and over again been disproved by the outcome.[12]

What the student of the fall of empires can say about the past is that, after power has been dispersed, the difficulty of living with

11. Michael Howard, *The Lessons of History* (Oxford: 1991).
12. The value of historical studies has never been better expressed to my knowledge than by the American historian of culture, Jacques Barzun, in an address entitled 'History Is Past and Present Life', delivered in 1984, reprinted in Jacques Barzun, *The Forgotten Conditions of Teaching and Learning* (Chicago: 1991).

the chaos gives opportunities for new empire-builders to arise. But we have no experience of empire-building in an era when weapons of mass-destruction are available both to impose hegemonies and to resist them. Tocqueville's prescience in forecasting the ultimate domination of the world by the United States and Russia has been much lauded. Yet, given the measuring rods of power available in the first half of the last century, it was not difficult to reach such conclusions. We now see how the differences between the two societies and the asymmetry of their capacities has made it hard to assess where they actually stand in relation both to mobilization of power and to its exercise. If I believed the United States was capable of prudent handling of the problems of empire, I would be more optimistic than I am. But what can one expect of a country to which isolation is natural, in which private concerns and private virtues are exalted above the public weal and in which, above all, the study of history is neglected for that of social sciences? To do good in the world one must first know it, and that must mean knowing its past.

Relics of empire persist in various ways. If Britain and France had not been world powers at the end of the Second World War, even if much diminished in relative strength by its impact, they would not be occupying permanent seats in the Security Council of the United Nations, as they did in the Council of the League of Nations between the wars. If one were constructing a Security Council from scratch at the beginning of the 1990s it would probably look very different. Attentive readers of this book may have noted that neither the League of Nations nor the United Nations have figured among my subjects of study.[13] The League of Nations never seemed more than a compromise between those properly anxious to improve communications between sovereign states so as to minimize the likelihood of conflict and those who believed that it should have coercive power to exercise against a potential aggressor. As a world organization, it lost credibility from the moment the United States repudiated President Wilson and refused to become a member. Reduced to a European role, it made very little difference to the course of events.

13.   In a series of lectures, planned in Delhi, written in Canberra and delivered in Montreal in 1967, I included a lecture on 'International Organizations: Records and Prospects'. After a quarter of a century, my approach in this area remains the same. See Max Beloff, *The Balance of Power* (Montreal: 1967).

The United Nations was a more deliberate attempt to carry over the successful wartime combination into a system for keeping the peace in the post-war world. The Charter was again a compromise between various schools of thought in the major countries. What it conspicuously failed to provide for and could not provide for was a similarity of objectives between the major participants, since they began with different ideological preconceptions. And this became even more obvious when Communist China was admitted to the fifth permanent seat on the Security Council. Gulfs between the interests of powers can always be bridged with or without the lubricating role of an international institution. Moral gulfs are harder to tackle. Where moral differences and material differences coincide, no organization can function successfully and any appearance to the contrary is likely to be short-lived. Historians explain and define such differences. That is their primary task.

# Bibliography of Books and Articles by Max Beloff

*Books*

*Public Order and Popular Disturbances, 1660–1714* (London, 1938)

*The Foreign Policy of Soviet Russia, 1929–1941*, 2 vols (London, 1947, 1949). Trans. *La Politica Estera della Russia Sovietica*, 2 vols (Florence, 1955)

*Thomas Jefferson and American Democracy* (London, 1948). Trans. *Thomas Jefferson e la Democracia Americana* (Rome, 1958); *Thomas Jefferson y la Democracia Norteamericana* (Mexico City, 1966); Hindi Translation (1960)

*Soviet Policy in the Far East, 1944–1951* (London, 1953). Trans. Japanese (Tokyo, 1953); Chinese (Hong Kong, n.d.), (Taipei, n.d.)

*The Age of Absolutism, 1660–1815* (London, 1954)

*Foreign Policy and the Democratic Process* (Baltimore, 1955)

*Europe and the Europeans* (London, 1957). Trans. *Europa und die Europäer* (Cologne, 1957); *L'Europa e gli Europei* (Milan, 1960); *Europa e Europeus* (Lisbon, n.d.)

*The American Federal Government* (London, 1959; 2nd edn, 1969)

*New Dimensions in Foreign Policy* (London, 1961). Trans. *Neuen Dimensionen der Aussenpolitik* (Cologne, n.d.)

*The United States and the Unity of Europe* (Washington, DC, 1963)

*The Balance of Power* (Montreal, 1967)

*The Future of British Foreign Policy* (London, 1969)

*Imperial Sunset*, vol. 1: *Britain's Liberal Empire, 1897–1921* (London, 1969; New York, 1970. 2nd edn, London, 1987; New York, 1988), vol. 2: *Dream of Commonwealth, 1921–1942* (London and New York, 1989)

With Gillian R. Peele, *The Government of the United Kingdom* (London, 1980; 2nd edn, 1985)

*Wars and Welfare: Britain, 1941–1945* (London, 1984)

*Collected Essays and Lectures*

*The Great Powers* (London, 1959)
*The Intellectual in Politics and Other Essays* (London, 1970)


*Works Edited*

*Mankind and His Story* (London, 1948)
*The Federalist* (Oxford, 1948; 2nd edn, 1987)
*The Debate on the American Revolution* (London, 1949; 2nd edn, 1960; 3rd edn,
   Dobbs Ferry, NY, 1989)
With P. Renouvin, F. Schnabel and F. Valsecchi, *L'Europe du XIX et du XX
   Siècle*, 7 vols (Milan, 1959–67)
*On the Track of Tyranny* (London, 1960)


*Uncollected Papers*

(This list omits many shorter pieces, particularly book reviews, a large proportion
   of which appeared in *Encounter.*)
'Return Journey', *The Pauline* (Summer, 1932).
'Humphrey Shalcrosse and the Great Civil War', *English Historical Review*, LIV
   (1939)
'A London apprentice's Notebook, 1703–1705', *History* n.s. xxvii (1942)
'Some Aspects of Anglo-Soviet Relations', *International Affairs*, XXI (April 1945)
'Law and Government in the U.S.S.R.', in J. L. Brierley (ed.), *Law and
   Government in Principle and Practice* (London, 1948)
'1848–1948: A Retrospective', in George Woodcock (ed.), *A Hundred Years of
   Revolution* (London, 1948)
'Great Britain and the American Civil War', *History*, n.s. xxxvii (1952)
'Russia', in A. Goodwin (ed.), *The European Nobility in the Eighteenth Century*
   (London, 1953)
'The Fourth Republic, 1945–1955,' in J. M. Wallace-Hadrill and J. McManners
   (eds), *France: Government and Society* (London, 1957)
*The Tasks of Government*, Inaugural Lecture. (Oxford, 1958)
'Tocqueville et l'Angleterre', in *Alexis de Tocqueville: Livre du Centenaire* (Paris,
   1960)
'The British Background of American Constitutionalism', in P. F. Jones (ed.),
   *The Constitution of the United States* (Pittsburgh, 1962)
'Britain, Europe and the Atlantic Community', *International Organization*, XVII
   (1963)
'International Organization and the Modern State', *Journal of Common Market
   Studies*, II (1963)

'L'URSS et l'Europe', in Max Beloff *et al.*, *L'Europe du XIX et du XX siècle*, vol. 3/2 (Milan, 1964)

'American Independence in Its Constitutional Aspects', *New Cambridge Modern History*, vol. 8 (Cambridge, 1965)

'Le Rôle des Etats Unis dans la politique Europcénne', in Max Beloff *et al.*, *L'Europe du XIX et du XX siècle* vol. 3. 2. (Milan, 1967)

'Il problema di Roma nella politica della Gran Bretagna', *Atti del XLV Congresso di Storia del Risorgimento Italiano* (Rome, 1972)

*Israel among the New Nations* (London, 1972)

'The Whitehall Factor: The Role of the Higher Civil Service, 1919–1939', in G. Peele and C. Cook (eds), *The Politics of Reappraisal* (London, 1975)

'The Politics of Oxford Politics: An Undelivered Valedictory Lecture', *Political Studies*, XXIII (1975)

'Britain and Canada between Two World Wars: A British View', in R. Lyon (ed.), *Britain and Canada: Survey of a Changing Relationship* (London, 1976)

'The Think Tank and Foreign Affairs', *Public Administration* (1977)

*The Tide of Collectivism: Can It Be Turned?* (London, 1978)

*The State and Its Servants* (London, 1979)

'The End of the British Empire and the Assumption of World-wide Commitments by the United States', in W. R. Louis and Hedley Bull (eds), *The 'Special Relationship'* (Oxford, 1986)

'The View from St James' Square', *National Interest*, 16 (Summer 1988)

'The Impact of the French Revolution upon British Statesmanship', in C. Crossley and I. Small (eds), *The French Revolution and British Culture* (Oxford, 1988)

'The Crisis and the Consequences for the Conservative Party', in W. R. Louis and R. Owen (eds), *Suez 1956: The Crisis and Its Consequences* (Oxford, 1989)

'Fault Lines and Steeples: The Divided Loyalties of Europe', *National Interest*, 23 (Spring 1991)

'Churchill and Europe', in W. R. Louis and Lord Blake (eds), *Churchill* (Oxford, 1993)

# Index